CANDY'S
Girl

SHAREEN KING

Candy's Girl by Shareen King

Copyright © 2024

All rights reserved. No part of this book may be reproduced, stored in a retrieval system, or transmitted in any form or by any means, electronic, mechanical, photocopying, recording, or otherwise, without the prior written permission of the publisher or author.

Printed in the United States

Published By Pure Thoughts Publishing, LLC, Conyers GA

ISBN: 978-1-953760-37-1 Paperback

Table of Contents

FOREWORD v

ACKNOWLEDGMENTS ix

CHAPTER 1: The Precious Virgin Mary 1

CHAPTER 2: Superman Was My Father 9

CHAPTER 3: Breakfast of Champions 17

CHAPTER 4: Mama's Slap back Moment 25

CHAPTER 5: Don't Answer The Phone! 29

CHAPTER 6: Busted & Disgusted 35

CHAPTER 7: The Love of a Grandmother 41

CHAPTER 8: Unbreakable City Girl 55

CHAPTER 9: Your Life is a Highlight 61

CHAPTER 10: A Place to Breathe 67

CHAPTER 11: The Big Regrets 75

CHAPTER 12: Working with Tyra 81

CHAPTER 13: It's a Blizzard! 89

CHAPTER 14: From Candy's Girl to the King's Daughter 103

ABOUT AUTHOR 107

FOREWORD
by Dr. Marita Kinney

In a world where stories of resilience and faith are often overshadowed by tales of adversity, Shareen King's memoir, *Candy's Girl,* stands as a beacon of hope and a testament to the indomitable strength of the human spirit. It is with great pride and admiration that I, as the owner of Pure Thoughts Publishing, present this powerful narrative to you.

From the moment I first encountered Shareen's story, I knew it was one that needed to be shared with the world. Her journey is not just one of overcoming obstacles but of transcending them through an unwavering belief in the promises of God. Shareen's life has been marked by challenges that would have caused many to falter. Yet, through her steadfast faith and relentless determination, she has not only survived but thrived, turning her trials into triumphs and her pain into purpose.

As a multiple Emmy Award-nominated media producer and President and CEO of The King's Daughter Media, Inc., Shareen has built an impressive career marked by excellence and creativity. Her professional accomplishments speak volumes, but it is her personal journey, filled with heart-wrenching losses and daunting obstacles, that truly defines her character and strength. In *Candy's Girl,* Shareen opens the door to her world, revealing the deep faith that has guided her through every challenge and the resilience that has driven her success.

Working in the entertainment industry can be exhilarating, but it also comes with its own set of challenges. Shareen has seen it all. From working with high-profile celebrities to navigating the intense pressures of the media world, she has consistently found herself in situations that demanded not only professional expertise but also deep inner strength. That same strength is evident in this memoir.

What I find most inspiring about Shareen's story is her refusal to allow her past to define her future. Instead, she has used her experiences as a foundation upon which to build a life of purpose and fulfillment. Her story is a reminder to all of us that, no matter what we face, there is always a way forward if we keep our eyes fixed on the promises of God.

As you turn the pages of *Candy's Girl*, you'll be invited into Shareen's world—a world filled with both dazzling successes and hidden battles. You'll hear about her encounters with some of Hollywood's biggest names, but more importantly, you'll see how she leaned on her faith to navigate the ups and downs that come with such a demanding career.

This memoir is more than just a recounting of her career highlights; it's an intimate look at the heart and soul behind the accomplishments. It's a reminder that, no matter what stage we find ourselves on—whether in the spotlight or behind the scenes—faith and resilience are what truly carry us through. Shareen's story is a testament to the power of believing in something greater than yourself, and it serves as an inspiration to all who face their own battles, both seen and unseen.

Candy's Girl will resonate with anyone who has ever felt the weight of expectation, the sting of disappointment, or the joy of overcoming the odds. It's a book for those who need to be reminded that they are never alone in their struggles, and that with faith, all things are possible.

As you embark on this journey with Shareen, allow her story to inspire you, to remind you that even in the midst of life's toughest challenges, there is always a way forward. Her experiences, both in the entertainment world and in her personal life, are a shining example of how faith can transform not just a career, but a life.

With deep respect and admiration,

Dr. Marita Kinney, BCC, Msc.D
Owner, Pure Thoughts Publishing

ACKNOWLEDGMENTS

I don't know how I could have ever survived without my Titi Mom and Tio Dad. I love you both to the moon and back. You have my guiding light and the wind that God used to breathe on me to encourage and push me into my destiny. You both have been beyond a blessing to my life and have continuously loved me beyond my flaws. I can't ever repay you for the love and guidance you've given me, and continue to give me throughout my life. This book is not only dedicated to you both, but probably would have never have happened without your influence. For years, you have spoken life into me and begged me to write a book. Well, here it is and I thank you for being such a force in my life. Life is hard and filled with so many disappointments but you both have never stopped loving me and I am proud to call myself your daughter. I know you are proud of me and that fills me with so much joy. You both mean the world to me and I couldn't make it without your love for me. Thank you! To my brothers, all 4 of you! I love you all so much, I'm so proud to be your sibling. Know that I will always have your back, no matter where I am. You all make me so proud. To my big sister, Arlene, I love you and I'm so glad that we've reconnected and are building our way to the best sister relationship in the world. You're a great woman and I hope one day to open a restaurant because you can cook your tail off.

Oo-Oop, to all my Soror's of Delta Sigma Theta Sorority incorporated! I love you ladies, especially my Pi-Delta ladies! You ladies are my sisters for real. I can't do this life without you ladies. Tameka, Jenya, JoAnn, Laverne,

Malika, and my line sisters, Tasha, Cordie's, Charlotte, Siomara....no words! I love you all so much.

I'm thankful for my team of co-workers who are warriors and have helped me make it through the last 3 years, it has been a time. However, y'all held me down so hard, and I'm so grateful for your love, support, and encouragement. It meant so much to me, in the word of Kendrick Lamar, "They NOT like US". We got through an entire pandemic with love and support for one another, no one could ever describe what we mean to one another. I love y'all.

To all my gals, you already know how important our friendships are to me, my sister- friends. You all have been mentors, therapist, prayer warriors, an ear, a shoulder, and overall a safe place for me most of my life. Over twenty-five years of friendship. Evolyn, Nichole, Merylin, Sonya, Joyce, and so many others, if I leave a name out, I will get killed, so let me just stop there. Please don't charge it to my heart!

Leanne, you girl! I love you and thank you so much for directing me into the right direction with writing this book. If you didn't do it first, who knows if I ever would have done it. Ha! I'm always here for you. I thank everyone who has ever sent me an encouraging word or message, they have all meant the world to me. My life is grand and full of love and support, and I'm so grateful.

Buckle Up!

Before we dive in, I encourage you to approach this journey with an open heart and without judgment. While I hold a bachelor's degree in psychology and a master's in social work, I am not a practicing therapist. What I'm sharing here are my personal experiences and the strength I've drawn from my faith. My hope is that my stories will help you recognize how past pains might have impacted your life.

I don't have all the answers—I'm still a work in progress, continually growing and developing. What I've learned is that we often carry past hurts into our future, allowing them to influence our decisions and plans. Don't let your past pain dictate your choices or hold you back. It's a trick and a lie that can keep you in bondage. I hope you find ways to release grief, anxiety, regret, and resentment from your life. It's a process, and it starts with acknowledging and moving through these emotions.

I discovered that I was seeking love and value from others instead of giving it to myself. Major losses in my life led me to shift my focus to achieving and overextending myself, which became a way of seeking love and validation. I now realize that my worth is not tied to what I give or achieve. People pleasing often stems from a desire for control and avoidance of conflict. The most crucial discovery you can make is self-love, understanding and setting your boundaries. While you might not see this reflected in my stories, I hope you can recognize it in your own life.

Release any guilt or shame from your past. The enemy's goal is to silence us, but silence can hold you back from becoming the person God intends you to be. Corrie Ten Boom once said, "If you look at the world, you'll be distressed. If you look within, you'll be depressed. If you look at God, you'll be at rest." My hope is for you to find rest by turning to God for answers and peace.

This journey requires continuous effort, reflecting on your thoughts, processing them, praying, and repeating. The learning and growing never truly end, but the goal is to gain a new perspective on your own story. I hope my words of faith and reflective questions offer you clarity and tools for growth.

I am on a quest for peace, peace within my decisions and relationships. Seeking peace often brings joy in the process. Do it for yourself; you deserve peace, and it begins in your heart. Take care of your heart. We all have stories to tell, especially those of pain. Your story matters. I share mine to heal and to inspire others. God uses our stories to bring hope to others and demonstrate that pain does not prevent progress.

Are you ready to self-reflect? Ready to answer questions for yourself? I hope so. Grab a pen and jot down notes from this book. You are the only one who can improve your well-being. It's a practice that never truly ends.

Let's embark on this journey together—toward health, happiness, and self-worth!

Thank you for joining Shareen on this remarkable journey. To get a closer look into her world, we invite you to scan the QR code below. This will take you to a special photo gallery that captures beautiful moments from her life, offering a more personal glimpse into her story.

Enjoy exploring these treasured memories and celebrating the experiences that have shaped her along the way.

CHAPTER ONE

The Precious Virgin Mary

The sounds rang out so loud, "Bang, Bang, Bang" I heard a scream. Dear God, please whatever is happening, don't let anything happen to the Virgin Mary! The scream was loud, it woke me up out of my sleep. I could tell from the tone of the scream that there was a surprise transaction happening that took someone off guard. I couldn't tell if it was the sound of my mother's voice or not. In fact, I couldn't tell if it was a man or a woman. It was the middle of the night and I was in bed. I grabbed the Virgin Mary statue, yes, the Virgin Mary statue, which is a story we'll get into later...so, I grabbed the statue and held her as tight as I could as I slid under my bed. All I could remember saying was "Jesus of Nazareth be with me", it was a saying that my Abuela taught me to say as a small child. I always felt like that phrase would protect me from anything and everything, because that is what she told me. I could actually hear Abuela's voice in my head saying it over and over again. For those who don't know, Abuela is grandmother in Spanish.

I was terrified, but not of the gunshots and the yelling I heard outside my bedroom door, but more so of something tragic happening to the statue that I had brought home from my school, Mary Help of Christians. The nuns and my classmates would never forgive me for bringing back a broken statue. How would I ever explain what happened to it? I couldn't face the nuns at Mary Help of Christians School if anything happened to the Virgin Mary statue. It was beyond an honor and a privilege to be given the responsibility of caring for the statue. In fact, I waited all school year long to be chosen to take the Virgin Mary statue home with me, it was a covenant opportunity for a one student to have the responsibility over the weekend to take care of the Virgin Mary and waiting over half the school year, I finally was seen as an "excellent student" and given this honor. That Friday, my name was called and our teacher, who was a nun, picked up the statue and said, you will be responsible for her this weekend. Spend time with her and take care of her, she said. I was smiling from ear to ear with excitement. Finally! I thought, I 'll get my chance. Someone is recognizing that I am special enough to take on this responsibility.

And of course, as it would in any dysfunctional family, all hell breaks loose the one time something magical happens for me. So, I was about 5 years old and I really don't know what exactly was happening in the rest of the apartment, but it didn't sound good. Whenever you just hear yelling and gunshots, that can't be a good sign. Like I said, the best thing I could do was grab Mary and slide under the bed, as I went down under the bed. I didn't even want the dust to touch her, so I tried to hold her up from the floor. Then, I realized I heard someone say "Police"! So, the police decided to raid my mother's apartment. So, now the Virgin Mary and I are involved in a full-blown shot-out on the lower east side.

Why does this stuff feel like it only happens to me? I'm so furious with this entire evening of events. I'm just praying for this all to be over quickly. I pray to Jesus of Nazareth and I'm asking him to rescue us from this moment in time. I wasn't as concerned for my siblings, as much as I was concerned for Mary.

How could I go back to school that Monday and explain to the nuns, who for sure already disliked my mother, which I knew for sure, after one nun made a point to let me know exactly how she felt about my mother. You know, till this day, I don't know why adults feel the need to share how they feel about other adults with small children. Anyway, this statue wasn't going to break or even worse, get a bullet hole put in it ... not on my watch! I couldn't imagine explaining that to my entire class. So, I wrapped her up as tight as I could in my pajama dress and I pulled my knees up to my chest while laying under my bed. Then, I remember my mother coming into the room, yelling "don't come out, until I come and get you!" Well she didn't have to worry because I wasn't going to move!

What was probably about thirty minutes felt like hours had passed, before I could come out of that room. I could hear a lot of shuffling and movement, it sounded like there were more than 100 people in the apartment, running up and down the hallway. And, although I was happy when that door opened, it became a real possibility that I may never see my mother again. That thought just froze me in time. The woman I cared the most about in life, my mother, was in danger, and I didn't really understand why. Please Lord, protect my mother and keep her from harm. Please, please, please, was all I could think. The door opens and she wasn't the one who opened the door, it was a police officer wearing a bulletproof vest. While holding on to the door open, he walks in and says out loud, "I got kids in this room. He said, "It's ok, you can come out." And so as careful as I could, I slid out from under the bed making sure I didn't scratch the statue in any way against the floor. I definitely didn't care about messing up my pj dress. I come out and stand up, the first thing I do is look at Mary to make sure she's ok. That moment was such a sign of relief. She made it through! Now, the next thought was where is my mother? The officer grabbed me by the shoulder and said, it's ok to come this way.

In my mind, I'm thinking, dude... I know this apartment better than you! I know which way to go! He walks me through the hallway, which at the time felt like it was 100 feet long. It was kind of a railroad apartment, where you have a very long hallway and every couple of feet there's a room on one side, or the other. Every time we passed a room, I would turn my head to see if I could see anyone, specifically looking for my mother. We got all the way down to the last room, and still no mom.

As we came upon the kitchen, I remember looking to my right and seeing several cops sitting at our kitchen table. I only assumed there were police officers, because they didn't have any uniforms on. They were all sitting there talking to one another and looking pretty impressed with one another. I think I noticed a smile or two on their faces, not sure at the time what they could be so happy or excited about.

There were piles of money sitting on the table and they were all focused on counting all the money. As the officer walked me out the door, I wasn't really sure where he was taking me. We got to the entrance of the apartment and there were some officers holding up the elevator, still not sure of what was happening. I remember the officer saying, we're going to the stairs and he even says, "bringing the kids down". I remember as we got to the staircase, the thought started to sink in that maybe my mother was dead. I had no idea of what was happening and why it was all happening. As we turned the corner on our way down the staircase, I started walking down the stairs and just a few steps down and I noticed there was a body on the floor. I don't think I recognized who he was, but it was the first time I had ever seen a dead body. Little did I know that I would see more dead bodies in the next few minutes. It shocked me right at the moment, I thought to myself was this my mother on the floor? I still had no idea. I needed to know, was it her? Thank God it wasn't my mother. There was a large pool of blood on the floor surrounding the body, terrified to look, but I did because I needed to know who its war. Was it her? I eventually realized the body belonged to a man. What man, I really didn't know. All I could think was thank God it wasn't her. The most horrifying part was we had to actually walk past the body, but it was the only way to get to the next level of the staircase going down.

I remember being so horrified at the pool of blood that was on the floor that I immediately started to cry. Up until that point, I felt like I had been strong. I didn't shed a tear or make a sound, but at that very second, I couldn't take it anymore. The thought of my mother possibly being dead just intensified and scared the life out of me. As we turned the corner, The officer continued to hold my shoulder and walk me down the 3 more flights of stairs. And as he opened the front door of the building, I could see that there was another body laid out on the concrete. Another man, who apparently was either thrown or shot and fell out of my mother's bedroom window. I couldn't believe what I was seeing and this was all happening in real life.

I remember the officer handing me off to someone. At the time, I couldn't tell you who the person was, and where I was going, but I ended up in my dad's house, which was a few blocks away. My mother and father were not an item at the time of this incident, but they didn't live far from one another, and so, I could only assume that it was my dad who came and got me and took me back home with him. I don't remember even asking about my mother, I think I was afraid to actually find out the truth. I didn't have that type of courage to know.

I can't really remember exactly how I got the rest of that weekend was kind of a blur. However, I do remember making it back to school Monday morning with the Virgin Mary, as if nothing ever happened. After wanting all year long to get the chance to be selected to take this statue home, I couldn't wait to get her out of my hands and put her back on in our class. As soon as I walked into the classroom, I walked straight to the desk and placed the statue on my teacher's desk with a sigh of relief. I went and sat down at my desk without any of my other classmates having a clue of the type of weekend I just went through.

Our teacher started our lesson plan and the rest of the day, I played with my friends and did whatever a 5-year-old does during a day at school. I don't remember not one person asking me a question about what happened or how I felt. It was business as usual. And, I think that was the day that I really understood that my mother was involved with bad people and that she was part of some type of drug cartel or business. This event was eye opening for me, and I understand that my life was a bit different from other kids. I did eventually find out that my mother was fine. I can't remember exactly when that was, but I can only imagine that she was taken to jail or held at the precinct, who knows. Again, it's not like anyone was ever going to have a conversation with a 5-year-old about it.

I find that very strange in retrospect that no one thought that maybe they should have a conversation with me, or maybe they did and I don't remember. This was the beginning of me learning that my family wasn't really the type to talk about a lot of things. And I learned to just keep things to myself and to continue to live life, regardless of what happens to you. This method of dealing with tragedy would follow me throughout my life and prevent me from being able to open up to people. I learned to process and deal with things on my own. The only person I ever learned to talk to was

God. That one lesson from my Abuela telling me to ask Jesus of Nazareth to be with me, becomes the blueprint of how I will deal and manage my life. And when I think about God's timing, I realized that God knew exactly when I needed to take the statue home with me.

God knew I needed that protection that weekend, and I learned that regardless of what is happening around me, I will come out on top. I made it through that weekend without a scratch on me, or the Virgin Mary statue.

C. S. Lewis once said "hardships often prepare Ordinary People for an extraordinary destiny." Life can be filled with a number of hardships and challenging situations but just know that God is always preparing you for an extraordinary destiny, as he did me. As you continue to read this book, you will hear story after story greater than myself, my God was always carrying me through.

Reflection of faith:
Whenever you are overwhelmed by life, retreat to prayer. Invited God to come into your life to help lead you through the dark places of life. Prayer works.

"Prayer is the place of refuge for every worry, a foundation for cheerfulness, a source of constant happiness, a protection against sadness." St. John of Chrysostom

"Who comforts us in all our affliction, so that we may be able to comfort those who are in any affliction, with the comfort with which we ourselves are comforted by God. 2 Corinthians 1:4

Sometimes the things we go through in life are not just for us, they are for the people who we may be assigned to help. Your testimony may be to help someone else.

The thing that I remember about this event in my life was that I never felt worthy to be trusted with the statue because I felt like my life was so unholy and filled with things that would not be honorable to God. ...but what I know now is that God will use the most unexpected people to do his work. God chose a prostitute, God chose a man who had a stutter, God chooses the most unlikely people to be used. I feel like in this experience, God learned that he could trust me because I valued the statue, because of the honor I have for God. What do you pay attention to? What do you show to God that you value in life? Is there something that doesn't deserve your attention, that you are giving too much attention to?

That is the beauty in God's grace, you don't have to be qualified to be used by God.

CHAPTER TWO

Superman Was My Father

I grew up on the Lower East Side of Manhattan, a place we called home for many years and still do in spirit. The L-E-S holds a special place in my heart, and I'll always have an affinity for it. I knew every street, every shop, and especially where to get the best slice of pizza. There was this little hole-in-the-wall spot on Avenue A, and even now, I can still smell that pizza. The shop was lined with bottles of oregano and pepper flakes, and a slice was always just a dollar. Sometimes, they'd even toss in a free fountain drink. I lived for that pizza, which is probably why I still love it today. It was my favorite after-school meal.

Then there was the penny candy shop on 12th Street and Avenue A, right next to my elementary school. The hustle was real there! I can still recall the smell of the store, dried-up caramels, Mary Janes, gumdrops, butterscotch sticks, Chick-O-Sticks, peanut chews, jawbreakers, and Tootsie Rolls. Those candied cherry hearts were always stuck together, and the chocolate squares in foil wraps kept you guessing—was it just chocolate or did it have Rice Krispies inside? I knew every dispenser in that store and exactly where to find my favorites. The brown paper bags waiting at the front of the store were like a ticket to candy heaven. I'd fill them up with all the candy I wanted, and I never spent more than seventy-five cents. It was a small shop, but it was packed with sweets. Visiting that store was my favorite after-school activity—sometimes even during lunch if I could sneak out with a few daring friends.

My father had a sweet tooth too. Veniero's, an Italian bakery on 11th Street and 1st Avenue, was his go-to spot. I think it's still there today. The smell of sugar in that place was unforgettable. Veniero's sold the best cookies in the world—an East Village staple since 1894! My dad was notorious for getting all our birthday cakes and treats from there. Sometimes, we'd stop by just to pick up a dozen Italian cookies. I loved the butter cookies with the chocolate drop in the middle, and even the marzipan cookies with their pink, green, and yellow dyes topped with chocolate. Their cannolis were the best I'd ever tasted. My dad had a thing for their strawberry shortcakes and would drive an hour just to pick one up. Watching them construct those white pastry boxes, tying them up with a red string in a perfect bow, was like watching art in motion. Nothing but joy. I loved my neighborhood, and my neighborhood loved me back. I guess this was the beginning of my love for food.

In the neighborhood, I was known as "Alvin's daughter." It was strange to be recognized solely by my father's name, but I understood his reputation—no one bothered him or anyone connected to him. My dad was an Afro-Rican, a mixed baby, half Black and half Puerto Rican. From what he shared, fitting in was a challenge; he was never Black enough for the Black crowd or Spanish enough for the Rican crowd. This made him tough, and he had to stand up for himself. He wasn't one to be messed with! As one of the elder brothers of 6 siblings. siblings, he took his responsibilities seriously. This forced my dad to feel responsible for filling his dad's shoes and being a protector of the household for his family. My aunts and uncles often told stories about how he was always there to protect them. He reminded me of a Robert DeNiro type—small in stature but larger than life. My dad carried a lot of trauma that he didn't know how to deal with, and showing strength was his way of coping.

His father, my grandfather, abandoned him, my aunts, and uncles when they were kids. My grandfather had another family, and when my abuela found out, their marriage was over. This forced my dad to step up as the head of the household for a family of seven. He loved his mother and siblings dearly and became their protector. No one in the community could harm them without facing my dad.

That's why, when people saw me, they'd say, "That's Alvin's daughter"—a warning for those who didn't know. My dad would send me to the store to buy his 40 oz of Ballantine Ale, and they'd sell it to me every time, even though I couldn't have been more than seven or eight years old. It's a familiar experience for anyone who grew up in a neighborhood where everyone knows your name and who you belong to. I ran around those streets like I owned them, without a trace of fear. We lived in a building owned by my godfather, Bernard, at 346 East 10th Street, apartment 4D. The number "4" has always been significant in my life, but that's a story for later.

Our apartment felt custom-made because my dad was a master carpenter who built a lot of things in our home. We had the only mahogany wood door in the building, with gold numbers and a knob. My dad built a platform in our kitchen, custom shelves in every room, and even my bed. As a kid, I didn't fully appreciate his talent and skill—I thought everyone's dad could do these things. We had shutter doors for the bedroom and a unique sofa bed in the living room that he also built. When guests stayed over, that's where they slept. My dad was incredibly skilled and gifted; I wish he were still around today to help me. But at least I have the memories of his craftsmanship.

Bernard, a masterful tailor, would make me custom outfits all the time, especially for me and my dad. Another one of my dad's best friends, Shannon, was a celebrity chef who also lived in our building. They both hosted many dinner parties in their apartments, for me as a kid it felt like my version of the famous Studio 54. Bernard also owned a nightclub downstairs attached to the building, for what I know from my aunts, it was the place to be. Shannon was a private chef for several celebrity kids. I felt grown-up because my dad was always working and I'd often have dinner with Bernard or Shannon, who both could cook, but I loved going to Shannon's mostly because he would always invite me to help make the meals. All my friends from elementary school lived within walking distance, and as a latchkey kid, I could go over to anyone's house, until my dad would get home from work, then my behind better be home. That was a joy for me

My dad was a sharp dresser, always in a well-put-together outfit. He loved a leather blazer and never just threw something on. For the early years of my life, these two men became like godfathers to me, and the entire building felt like a family. Bernard owned the building, and everyone in it was more than just neighbors. These two men played significant roles in my life, and I'll always be grateful to them for the time they invested in me. They were the only two men I trusted to take care of me when my father couldn't. They loved me like their own child.

The park across the street, where my father played basketball with the locals, was where we spent most of our free time. The library was also across the street from the park. I loved going there to study or do homework. The 10th Street library was a playground for me, with books, events, games, there was always something to do. It made me feel independent, like a teenager. My elementary school was only two blocks away, so I walked everywhere. To this day, people tease me because I love walking everywhere, a habit that started in childhood. As an adult, I could walk from 14th Street to 125th Street without a second thought. I enjoy being outside, walking, and people-watching. One thing I always hated as a New Yorker was taking the train. I guess as a child, I walked and rode the bus everywhere, so I still prefer that over taking the train.

Anyway, I loved this neighborhood, and these were my people. I knew every area and every building. I couldn't imagine leaving as a child. In my mind, I thought I'd always live there.

My dad was like a superhero to me—always there, always protecting, always making sure we had fun, nice clothes, and spent time with family. He was a great provider who never missed a day of work. EVER. He was a great dad, and it wasn't until he was gone that I realized how special and unique he was as a man and a father.

One time, when I was in the park on the swings, someone started to push me higher and higher. At first, it was fun, but then it got too high, and I started to scream for them to stop. They just laughed and kept pushing. My dad was playing pickup basketball on the courts, but he heard my screams. I remember him running across the park, jumping over the fence that divided the courts from the swings. Just as I was about to fall out of the swing, he caught me in mid-air and stopped the swing. I don't know how he got across that park so fast, but like I said, he was a superhero to me. He wasn't very tall, maybe five-foot-seven or eight, but what he lacked in height, he made up for in stature.

Another time, we were dropping my brother off at his mother's house. My dad and I were walking down about six flights of stairs when we reached the bottom, where there was a double glass door that needed to be buzzed open. We tried to open the door, but it was stuck. At the same time, a group of firefighters came into the lower level of the building. They wanted to get in, so they asked us to open the door. My father pulled on the door, but it still wouldn't budge. He yelled to them, "It's stuck!" The firefighters started yelling at him to open the door, but he shouted back, "Didn't you hear me? It's stuck!" The firefighters ran towards us and started shoving the door, and finally the door opened. It was a huge commotion. My dad pulled me behind him, and within seconds, he was on the floor after leaping off the steps on top of the firefighters. Shortly after that, he was being handcuffed by the firefighters.

"Get off my dad!" I screamed.

"You're hurting him!" But they didn't care. They tossed me aside and arrested him right in front of me.

They took us both to the precinct. It felt like a bad dream. I just wanted to wake up and forget it ever happened. But it was real. Eventually, I remember my Uncle coming to get us, and they let us go, but that day changed me. I saw how quickly things could escalate with my dad in real time, he was not to be played with.

Reflection of Faith:
There are times in life when you may feel let down or disappointed by your family, but I've learned that those moments pale in comparison to the ones that bring joy. The memories I hold of my father and other family members who are no longer here are precious. It doesn't matter when I felt hurt or

upset; what truly matters is the time I was able to spend with them. Those cherished moments become the most important because, once they are gone, all you have left are the memories. You won't get any new ones, and that can be a hard reality to accept. The impact they had on your life, their deposits of love and wisdom, will be their lasting gift—so treasure them.

Take what you can from those relationships and learn from them. Spend time with the people you love, because they won't be here forever. One day, they will be gone, and you don't want to live with regrets about missed opportunities to connect. If you love the Lord and seek to honor Him, surrender any feelings of anger toward one another.

1 John 4:20 says, "Whoever claims to love God yet hates a brother or sister is a liar. For whoever does not love their brother and sister, whom they have seen, cannot love God, whom they have not seen."

This revision keeps the original heartfelt message while refining the language for clarity and flow.

CHAPTER THREE

Breakfast Of Champions

My mother and father were never really an item. They could never seem to get along, or so I was told. Both were Scorpios, born in November, and they both had a stinger, each loved to sting. Despite my mother being a bit older, their personalities clashed, and their seed (me) inherited both of their stingers, ha! "Don't cross me; it won't go well for you," I've often been told. However, I'm also the sweetest person you'll ever meet, so I don't know.

As a child, I went back and forth between my parents, but I spent a lot more time with my dad than with my mother. After some unfortunate events in our Lower East Side (LES) apartment, my mother decided to move us to Brooklyn. I wasn't thrilled. I remember thinking, "Why in the world do we have to go to Brooklyn? What could possibly be there for us?"

We arrived, and my mother parked the car. We all got out and walked over to the building. I followed her as she led the way. Maybe we were visiting a friend of hers; she knew so many people. But when she whipped out a set of keys and unlocked the door, I looked at her in disbelief. Low and behold, this was our new place, a first-floor railroad apartment. I had no idea we had moved.

As strange as it may sound for a kid to say, I belonged in Manhattan. I was a NYC kid, not a Brooklyn kid. I always thought I would live on the LES. I knew every inch of the neighborhood, but Brooklyn? I was like the kid version of Miranda in *Sex and the City*, wondering who lives in Brooklyn! I was used to being able to go outside and head over to the park or the grocery store by myself, or grab a slice of pizza. Now, here I was in Flatbush. Jesus, be a fence.

Thank God I knew this might just be for the weekend, because I'd be heading back to my dad's place in a few days. I knew everyone in my neighborhood, and more importantly, they knew me. How many times had I heard, walking down the street, "That's Alvin King's daughter, don't talk to her." That was my safe place. But Brooklyn seemed like a world away, completely foreign to me.

It wasn't long before we were all set up in our new apartment. There were times when my mother didn't feel like driving to the city, so I'd stay home from school. I never took the train or bus to school. On this particular day, though, my mother had other plans, or maybe she just needed an extra pair of hands. I didn't care why, I was just happy to spend the day with her.

After breakfast, she told me she needed my help with a project.

Now, let me tell you about this breakfast. My mother made the fluffiest scrambled eggs I'd ever had, with cheese and peppers. To this day, I still love creamy scrambled eggs, and I'm sure my love for them started with her. She would make toast with mounds of butter splattered on it. Then there was this drink, a mix between milk and orange juice, something like an orange creamsicle. I later found out it was probably a popular Dominican drink called Morir Sonando, a delicious morning milkshake with ice, carnation milk, and orange juice. I'm not sure of the exact ingredients, but it was one of the best things my mom ever made. Funny enough, it's the only meal I can vividly remember her making.

With our tummies full, it was time to start our project. My mom prepped the coffee table in the living room, gathering supplies, including a few rolls of aluminum foil. "You're going to be my helper today," she said. I was excited to spend the day with her, even more eager to see what this project was all about.

She began cutting the aluminum foil into squares, piling them up. "We're going to layer these sheets of foil," she explained. Once everything was lined up perfectly, we cut them into small squares. She showed me how to do it, and soon we were sitting on the floor, cutting foil squares together.

It felt like an arts and crafts project, just the two of us, smiling and working. She complimented my foil-cutting skills, and staying home that day didn't seem so bad. After some time, we had stacks of foil squares ready. Then she pulled out a substance that looked like white flour and poured it into a bowl.

"This part is tricky," she said, handing me a small spoon, about the size of a sugar spoon. "You have to be careful. Take just enough to fill the spoon, then dump it in the center of the foil square." She showed me how to fold the foil, making sure it was tight. I watched her closely, not wanting to mess it up. "You're doing a great job, baby," she encouraged.

We spent hours filling and wrapping the foil squares, taking breaks to watch TV or grab a snack. Eventually, we had nothing but little foil packets on the table, almost like pieces of gum. Just when I thought we were done, she said, "Now we have to pack these into bundles."

"What's that, Mom?" I asked.

She explained that we would take ten pieces of the wrapped foil, line them up, and roll them into something she called a "bundle." The process continued until every piece of foil was packed into a bundle. By the end of the day, I was exhausted. That was the first and last time I remember doing this in my life. I have no idea where those bundles went, but my fingerprints were on every single one of them.

I never really shared that story until now, but as an adult, it shows me that my mother had no sense of what was appropriate for a child to know. She demonstrated that several times in my childhood. Like the time she asked me to take pictures of her in lingerie to send to her boyfriend who was in jail. I couldn't have been more than five or six years old, snapping pictures of her posing on her bed. It's a strange memory that will likely never leave me.

Another day, another school day, my mother came into my room and asked, "Do you want to go with Mommy today?"

"Of course!" I replied. "Where are we going?"

"We're going to visit a friend of mine," she said. "Hurry up and get dressed."

I got ready quickly, and she made sandwiches for our trip. We headed to Penn Station, and I was thrilled—it was a private adventure, just the two of us. I remember looking out the window, watching the roads and fields, wondering where we were headed.

Finally, we arrived at the bus station, but I still had no idea where we were going. When I asked again, she told me we were visiting her friend, Manolo, a man she had been dating for a while. I had no idea he was in prison. We boarded the bus along with other women and children, all heading to the same place.

As the bus pulled up to the gates, we got off and formed a line. The guards instructed us to remove our shoes and other items. I was scared—I had never been to a prison before. As we were escorted to a table, I couldn't understand why we were there. When Manolo walked into the room, my mother was so happy to see him. I was not. She sent me to get some snacks from the machine, and as I stood by the window, staring at the fields, I felt like we were in a foreign place.

Back at the table, Manolo tried to grab my hand, but I pulled away. I didn't consider him a friend or someone who truly cared for me. I think he was just trying to impress my mother. I occupied myself with coloring books while they visited, and before I knew it, until it was time to head back on the bus, heading to the train station.

So, sidebar about Manolo, I never saw him as a good man. When he came into my mother's life, she changed. I was very young at the time, but I do blame him for the presence of drugs in our life. He was also a very fresh man, and I don't mean, he smelled fresh. One day, I was in the kitchen looking out the window waiting for my dad to pick me up. My mom was not at home. Manolo was in the shower and he was done. I could hear his feet walking down the hall towards the kitchen. I felt a very eerie feeling come over me and so I clinched the child protection bars that were bolted to our window and held them for dear life. I didn't know what was going to happen. He entered into the kitchen in his towel and stood behind me. I was terrified to turn around so I squeezed the bars even harder. Before I knew it, I could feel the wind of his towel hit the floor. I was paralyzed. He stood there in silence. It was a defying silence that felt like hours. After some time, he began to press his body up against my backside. I could feel his bare body on me...and within that moment tears just ran down my face. I could see my dad come around the corner and I just ran out of the apartment as quick as I could. I didn't even wait for the elevator. When I got to my dad, I just hugged him. I didn't say a word because I knew he would kill him. I didn't want him to go to jail, so I never said a word. So, yea... he wasn't a friend.

On the train, my mother looked at me and said, "Don't tell anyone where you were today."

"Okay," I replied, but that's when I felt the most disgusted. I assume that she was mainly talking about my dad, because again, he probably would have lost it if he knew we went to prison to visit some man. It was clear that this wasn't a place we should have been. So much for a great adventure with my mom!

Reflection of Faith:
I don't know what the lesson was at that moment, but I do know that the Bible says, "Honor thy mother and father, and your days shall be long." I tried hard to honor my mother's requests, sometimes to my own detriment. I try to honor those I love, but how do you honor yourself? How do you take care of yourself? Secrets can kill you—don't hold on to things that weigh you down. Sometimes you have to let go of what is killing you, even if it feels like it's killing you to let it go.

My mother only had the capacity to be the type of mother she was. I don't believe she ever had a good example of a mother. I didn't get to know her mom well, I only met her one time, so that in itself speaks volumes to me.

These were my mother's decisions, and they had nothing to do with me. People make decisions they believe are best for them. Don't judge someone's decision until you understand the context behind it. Think about a few secrets or things you need to release and let go of. Release them, and release the people you felt you were honoring by keeping those secrets.

Shareen King

CHAPTER FOUR

Mama's Slap back Moment

I attended Mary Help of Christians, a Catholic elementary school on the Lower East Side of Manhattan, at 12th Street and Avenue A. It's now a weekly flea market in the old schoolyard. This school laid the foundation for my faith and spiritual life. I started in pre-K and stayed until 6th grade. Though the school was great, I never felt comfortable around the nuns. Most of them terrified me, but a few were fun. I remember one time when I was waiting for my mom or someone to pick me up after school. Hours passed, and no one came. My father's house was only a few blocks away, but the nuns wouldn't let me leave.

The nuns took me to their convent around the corner. They sat me in a room alone and told me to do my schoolwork, which I did. After some time, they came to get me for dinner. The funny thing was, I didn't smell any food cooking. All I could smell was the scent of ashes from the church connected to the convent. The air was dry and plain; I couldn't imagine what dinner would be. They seated me at the table, and one of the nuns made me a basic plate of food, handing me a piece of bread. The nuns said grace and chatted among themselves but didn't speak much to me. I just stared at them while they talked.

After dinner, they asked me to help in the kitchen. I helped put dishes away, and then they escorted me back to the room where I had done my work. I don't remember there being a TV—just a desk and a bed. I wondered if I was going to have to sleep there. I lay on the bed, waiting for someone to come and get me. Finally, after what felt like an eternity, someone came and told me, "Your father is here." I was so relieved. I grabbed my bag and practically ran to the door. My father thanked the nuns, and we left. No conversation about what had happened, why I was there—just a quick exit, with him asking if I was hungry.

The following week was school picture day. My mother had spent the entire Sunday doing my hair. At that time, my hair reached down to my butt, thick and wavy. It took all day to wash and style it. Unlike most kids, I loved getting my hair done. My mom decided to put my hair in small box braids, with barrettes and colorful rubber bands. I thought I looked cute. She took her time, making all my parts even. So, when Monday came, I was ready for my class photo.

When it was time for our class to take the picture, the principal, a nun, looked at me and asked, "Did your mother not know you were taking pictures today?" I replied, "Yes, she did. She did my hair like this all night." The nun frowned and said, "Well, that's not an appropriate hairstyle for pictures; we're going to take it out." Two nuns began untwisting my hair. When they were finished, they brushed it into a ponytail, which looked awful. If you've ever taken out twists, you know it leaves your hair big and frizzy. They stuck me in line with the rest of my class, and I took my class picture with that unruly hair.

When my mother picked me up from school that day, she was livid. "Who did that to you?" she demanded. I was terrified, I had never seen her that angry. I hesitated, but when she gave me a look, I blurted out, "It was Sister…" My mom parked the car, dragged me back into the school, and went straight to the nun's office. She had a few choice words for the nun before slapping her across the face. All I heard was, "If you ever touch her hair again…" I was beyond shocked, all I could think was, we're going to hell because my mother just slapped a nun.

As we walked back to the car, my mother bent down and said, "If you ever let someone touch your hair again, I'm going to slap you." I started to cry; I had never seen her so mad. The next day, I returned to school, and that nun saw me in the hallway. She had a few things to say about my mom, though I don't remember much. The one thing that stood out was her saying, "I know what your mother does," and she squeezed my arm as hard as she could. I definitely thought she was going to kick me out of school. My heart pounded with fear. I definitely wasn't going to tell my mother about that incident—I couldn't imagine what she would do next after slapping a nun. Though, I did want to slap that nun myself… off to confession I go!

School at Mary Help of Christians was always interesting. I distinctly remember being in the bathroom in second grade, with classmates who touched my hair and asked if I was Black or Puerto Rican. It's shocking that even at such a young age, these are the images and thoughts ingrained in children's minds. I never felt like I was Puerto Rican because most of my classmates were Spanish and looked different from me. Every girl had straight black or brown hair, while my hair was wild, period. Long and thick, it never seemed to be under control. I never realized how much that impacted my life. I never fully accepted my Spanish heritage because it was easier to explain that I was Black. I didn't speak Spanish, and I didn't have the looks of everyone else in the neighborhood. Growing up on the Lower East Side of Manhattan, was not as diverse as it is now. You were either Black or Spanish, and it definitely felt like our community was predominantly Latino community. I loved Spanish food, but I didn't speak the language, and my dad wasn't fluent in Spanish either. His mother's family was from Spain, and his father's family was African American.

For years growing up, I tried to dye, fry, and straighten my hair. I never accepted my curls until after college. It's amazing how something as simple as a girl touching my hair influenced the way I felt about myself. I spent many years judging my looks and my appearance because I never fit in with any one class of people. Being a mixed kid is not easy and my dad had the same challenge growing up. I think maybe if he had dealt with his own issues around being of mixed race, maybe he could has taught me a thing or two about it.

Reflection on Faith: Self-Esteem
Self-esteem is about recognizing your flaws but still holding yourself in high regard. Be mindful of how you view yourself, especially after someone tries to make you feel inadequate or less than. Your value and self-esteem should not be tied to what others say about you. Build yourself up. Don't hold on to labels others try to place on you, they aren't the truth. The truth is that God made you beautiful and wonderful. You are unique, special, and you need to believe that about yourself. It's a practice and a work in progress, it may not come naturally to boost yourself, but I promise you, you are special. Looks are surface-level and of little consequence; you can always change your appearance, so don't tie your self-esteem to that. Focus on developing who you are and how you want to be remembered. There is only one of you, there's no one else like you.

CHAPTER FIVE

Don't Answer The Phone!

It was a Friday, and I spent the entire day waiting for my mom to pick me up. She usually showed up at my school in her car or limo, but this day, she didn't come. I waited for a while after school, thinking she was running late. But after everyone else had left, I realized she wasn't coming, so I walked back to my dad's house, just a few blocks away. I expected her to call and explain, but that call never came.

When my dad came home, I kept asking if he had heard from her, but he hadn't. He insisted that I go to bed without watching TV, which was surprising, but I thought maybe he just wanted to hang out with his friends without me around. I stayed in my room, upset that my mother had stood me up. She had never done this before, and I couldn't understand why it was happening. I kept calling her house, but there was no answer. I was annoyed, where the heck was she? I started to think maybe she had left town without me, which made me even more upset.

The next morning, my dad was up early. He woke me up and asked me to pack a small bag with a change of clothes. When we went outside, the air felt so crisp, I remember it like it was yesterday. As we headed to our olive-green van, my dad said, "We're going camping with your uncle for the weekend." I was so excited, what kid doesn't love an impromptu weekend getaway? When we arrived at the campsite, it was practically empty, which I didn't understand at the time. Most parents don't take their kids camping in the middle of the school year. But we had fun, we made hot dogs and marshmallows, and on the first night, my dad decided to take a swim in the pool.

I think we jumped the fence because I don't believe it was even open for the season. Anyway, he dives into the pool in the dark and slams his head right into a wall. I've never seen a knot swell so fast; it made me so nervous. I just knew he was going to pass out, and then what? The next morning, we headed back home because my dad's head was hurting so badly.

When we arrived home, everything seemed normal, but when my dad left to go to the store, I was alone in the house. The phone rang three times before I picked it up. It was my little brother's mother. She said, "I'm so sorry to hear about your mother." I was confused, "What? What are you talking about? What's wrong with my mother?" "Oh," she said, "you don't know?" "Know what? What are you talking about?" "Your mother is dead," she replied. I screamed at her, "You're a liar! What's wrong with you? I hate you!" Then I hung up the phone.

She angered me like never before. We had an interesting past. We didn't have the best relationship. When I was a little girl and her and dad were living together, she hated to wash my hair. Like I mentioned earlier, my hair was long and kind of wild, so it would take a lot to wash and blow out. She was the first woman to ever cut my hair, and that didn't end well for her. One day, she got tired of washing it and decided to make one long braid and just cut it off. I've never heard my father yell at someone the way he yelled at her that day. Another time, she was upset that I wasn't listening to her. She made me kneel on a bed of raw rice as punishment. I had to stay there in the middle of the living room, naked, until my father came home. He was so shocked when he saw me. He yelled at me to get up immediately and go to my room and put some clothes on. My father had some very strong words for her about her decision to punish me in that way. To this day, I've never heard of or seen anyone do that to a child. It must have been something from her upbringing, but my father didn't agree with her methods.

Another time, she poured me a bowl of Cheerios, which I couldn't eat. Like old-school parents, she made me sit at the table until I ate it, but I couldn't, and when I tried, I threw up right into the bowl. She told me I was going to eat that cereal, vomit and all. To this day, I can't stand the smell of Cheerios, it makes me sick to my stomach!

My dad often shared his discontent with her methods, but he loved her, even though their relationship didn't work out. Needless to say, she was not the one I needed to hear this news from, and I didn't believe her! When my father arrived home, it was obvious that something was wrong. The TV was broken, the cushions from the couch were tossed on the floor, and I was crying on the floor with the phone hanging off the hook. He knew I knew. He asked, "Who called?" I told him it was Mary, and he just grabbed me while I cried so hard. I couldn't believe he didn't say it wasn't true. I was crushed. Life felt like it stopped moving that day. I would never be the same again.

The next few days are blank in my mind.

As for my mother's murder, the story I heard was that it was a drug war on 6th Street near a club she hung out at. It was a drive-by shooting between two parties, and my mother was killed in the crossfire. I don't know if she was targeted or just happened to be in the wrong place at the wrong time. Over the years, I've heard three or four different versions of what happened to her. One thing is for sure, the news articles all mentioned a drug war in the description of her death.

I remember my dad taking me with him to the morgue and he must have been going there to identify the body. I'm not sure as I was so young, but I can only assume that was what was happening. The morgue was located somewhere on First Avenue, maybe at Bellevue, but I'm not sure. When we arrived, I could still see the tan bricks on the outside of the building and the blue-green walls of the hallway inside. It was cold and icy, both in temperature and feeling. My dad told me to wait outside the door and not to move. I said okay, but the way he said it was so serious that I knew something was wrong. He went into a room, and although it was probably only a few minutes, it felt like hours to me. When he came out, he grabbed me and hugged me, then said, "Let's go home." He held my hand so tight without saying a word. We walked all the way home in silence.

I don't remember much of the next few days, but I do recall Bernard sewing an outfit for me to wear to the funeral. At first, I didn't think my dad was going to take me to the funeral, but at the very last minute, he did, for just a few minutes. The funeral home was only a few blocks away, so we walked there. My dad kept asking if I was okay. I said yes, but I don't think I fully understood what was happening. I remember taking a picture of myself at the funeral, planning to put it inside the casket. Once we arrived, I walked in and immediately started crying. I don't recall seeing anyone I knew, though they were likely there. I just don't remember. I placed my picture inside the casket, walked back to my dad, and we left. We walked home in silence again. I was in shock; I couldn't believe I would never see my mother again.

It was an awkward time, and I think my dad was trying hard to help me forget about my mother's death. We never had a conversation about her being killed or how I felt about it, not really the best thing to do, but it was what he knew at the time.

For him, helping me meant taking me away on a trip. He decided a weekend camping trip would be the best way to cope. He invited my Uncle George, who was also like my dad's best friend. They hung out all the time, maybe a bit too much. He was also my Godfather, and I enjoyed being with him. So, we went on this camping trip.

We arrived at night. There was a pool, and my dad knew I loved to swim. Not to brag, but I was in the Junior Olympics as a swimmer and won a bronze medal. I don't know if it was the real Olympics, but that's what they told us, so I'm going with it. Anyway, as I said, it was dark when we arrived, and my dad thought it would be a good idea to sneak into the pool area. The pool was closed, but that didn't stop us—we were rebels.

My dad and I began to climb over the fence. I don't remember if my uncle did, but my dad leaped over while I had to climb. We were at the pool, and at the end we were standing at, it said no diving. Well, my dad decided to dive right in, not noticing the wall dividing the shallow part from the deep part. He slammed his head into the wall, bam! I thought he was about to drown. He had the biggest bump on his head and cursed like a sailor. He asked me to go get my uncle, and if I remember correctly, that was the end of that weekend trip.

Reflection of Faith

I realized that my dad wasn't good at processing trauma or dealing with conflict. In fact, this event was a clear example of conflict avoidance, something my family often practiced. I didn't understand this until recently, but I now see that these moments were when I learned how to handle, or rather, avoid conflict. This became the start of a habit that would eventually cost me many relationships in life. I began to just go with the flow, never addressing the real issues at hand.

After my mom passed away, I learned to shut down emotionally. I convinced myself that it was okay to never express the difficult things. This pattern of avoidance has become a deeply ingrained habit, one I've been working hard to correct. Instead of confronting my feelings, I channeled that pent-up energy into pursuing achievements, adventures, and exploration, anything to avoid processing real emotions.

Take a moment to reflect on the ways you might have avoided conflict in your own life. Have you swept things under the rug? Have you gone along with the flow just to avoid ruffling any feathers?

When faced with conflict, it doesn't mean you have to attack someone. There is a healthy way to have a conversation about the things that are bothering you or that have caused you pain or discomfort. Conflict doesn't have to lead to destruction. In fact, it's an opportunity to build something meaningful. So don't be afraid to confront the problem head-on.

Scripture: "For God hath not given us the spirit of fear, but of power, and of love, and of a sound mind." - 2 Timothy 1:7

CHAPTER

SIX

Busted & Disgusted

My dad was an excellent carpenter and licensed steamfitter. He made so many things in our home, from the front door to the shutters on the windows, and even my bed. Our apartment had unique touches, like a platform in the kitchen for the dining table, and custom shelves in the living room for our record player and other items, all made by my dad. One day, I accidentally knocked a vase off the shelf, and a few small folded items fell out. They looked like strips of gum, but I quickly realized they were drugs. Instinctively, I took them to the bathroom and flushed them down the toilet. My dad walked in just as I was doing this, and he yelled, screamed, and pulled me by one arm out of the bathroom. I fell to the floor as he stuck his hand in the toilet, trying to retrieve the drugs. That moment was when I knew things were bad.

I don't remember when my dad started using drugs. He never missed a day of work and always provided for me. But after my mom's passing, he began drinking more and experimenting with other substances. My dad had unresolved feelings of abandonment from his father and never sought therapy. He struggled with not fitting into a community where he didn't belong. Perhaps all these emotions built up inside him until one day, he just couldn't cope anymore. Or maybe it was peer pressure, wanting to fit in, so he indulged in drugs and alcohol.

Suddenly, our apartment became a gathering place for my dad's friends and women. I say "hang out" loosely because they were doing much more than that. I would retreat to my room and watch TV or go upstairs to Shannon's or downstairs to Bernard's, whoever answered the door first. Sometimes, I would spend the night there, only returning home in the morning to get dressed for school. My dad left for work early, around 5 or 6 am, so I would walk myself to school, which as I mentioned before was just a few blocks away.

I started rebelling and didn't want to go to school anymore. I stayed home, watching TV all day, afraid of anyone seeing me. Like I mentioned earlier, people in my neighborhood knew who my father was, so they knew who I was. Between losing my mom and discovering my dad's drug use, I was overwhelmed and didn't have the maturity to talk to anyone about it, I was just a child. One day, while lying on the couch, I heard keys in the door. My heart sank, it was my dad coming home early from work. I quickly pretended to be sick, moaning and clutching my stomach. When he walked in, he asked, "What are you doing here?" I told him I wasn't feeling well and had stayed home. He didn't feel well either and went straight to the restroom. I thought I was safe. But when he came out, he told me to put on my shoes, we were going to my school.

I prayed silently as we walked the two blocks to my school. When we arrived, my dad asked the receptionist for a count of how many days I had been absent. The shock on my face must have been evident, but the receptionist turned to my dad and said, "12 days in a row." My heart sank as I looked at her like, you liar! We walked back home in silence; he didn't say a word or look at me. Once home, he told me to have all my homework and assignments ready. I assured him I did. He looked me straight in the eyes and said, "You better not ever miss a day of school again." To my surprise, there was no beating, just a stern warning. However, I was punished and wasn't allowed to hang out with anyone in the building.

My dad started coming home early more often, usually before I got back from school. At the time, I thought he was trying to catch me skipping school. In hindsight, I know it was because of his drinking and drug use. Things would get worse before they got better, for both of us.

The addiction and abuse escalated to the point where we lost our apartment. That was the hardest part because we knew everyone in the building, we were one big family. One day, I came home from school, and my keys didn't work in the door. Confused, I went to Shannon's apartment and told him I couldn't get in. I don't remember seeing my dad that day. Lucky for me, my father's sister lived a few blocks away, so all I remember is going to her house and spending the night there. That marked the end of my days on the Lower East Side.

I eventually went to stay with my Titi and Tio on the Upper West Side. My father needed time to get his life together. While he was figuring things out, I stayed with them. But that was short-lived because my dad would show up at their building, pounding on the windows and demanding to see me. My Titi, which means Aunt in Spanish, couldn't handle the harassment, so she sent me to my Abuela's house on 92nd and 1st Avenue. I stayed with her for a while, but it became too much for her too, as my dad continued to show up, upset that his family had taken me away. Eventually, my family decided to send me to California to live with my father's brother and his wife, Tio

Michael and Titi Pam. They thought this would be a safe place where my dad couldn't just show up unannounced.

Living with them in Pasadena was interesting. It was always sunny, and people seemed happy. I enjoyed spending time outside with my family and learned the art of making burritos since we ate a lot of them. My family were vegans, which was a new concept for me, coming from the Lower East Side, where I ate cuchifritos and blood sausages regularly. But I'm a foodie and love good food, so I adapted. Eventually, I was sent back to New York to live with my Abuela again. I spent most of my teen years with her until my dad got his life together. It was in the following years that I learned his drug use had exposed him to HIV, a consequence he would pay for severely later in life. But I'll get to that later.

Reflection of Faith:
Psalm 34:17 says, "The righteous cry out, and the LORD hears them; he delivers them from all their troubles." Some interpret this verse to mean that God always hears the cries of the righteous, no matter their circumstances. Others believe it's about the long game, God will deliver people from trouble because Jesus died on the cross for their sins.

If you ever feel desperate, like there's no hope, cry out to God, for He will never forsake you. He can remove your burdens, your bondage, your strongholds, whatever is weighing you down. God is the author and finisher of our faith. Addictions are hard to beat on your own; you need supernatural help to overcome them. It's more than just willpower. My father had the willpower to fight his addiction, but he learned that he needed God to push him through to healing and self-worth. Once he understood that, getting free from addiction was a done deal. He never went back and became an even better father and man than before. He showed me the power of strength and the ability to overcome. Like I said, he was built differently.

Shareen King

CHAPTER SEVEN

The Love of a Grandmother

Living with my Abuelita were some of the greatest years of my teenage life. I learned so many lessons from her that I still put into practice today. She was a petite woman with striking red hair and equally vibrant red nails, always speaking her mind. Despite her small stature, she was a titan. At just 17, she married to escape her home, had six children, and became a single mother, working tirelessly to support her family. On the Lower East Side, she was renowned for her role as a community leader and advocate. She was the driving force behind a community health center called "Nina," and collaborated with the Mayor's office, receiving numerous commendations for her work. That was my Abuela!

When I returned from California, the first priority was getting me enrolled in school. Abuela lived on 92nd Street and 1st Avenue, so a school on the East Side of Manhattan made sense. She decided on Wagner Junior High School, located on 75th Street. I remember the enrollment process vividly. I was told I needed to take an exam to determine my class placement. I've always hated tests—my anxiety around them made the experience physically painful. After spending an entire day taking multiple exams, the results came back, and we were asked to return to the school.

When we arrived, Abuela had a big smile, expecting them to tell her I was a prodigy. However, that wasn't the case.

"Ms. King, we've reviewed your granddaughter's exam results," the Principal said. "We're placing her in 7th grade, which is appropriate, but she will be in the third tier of classes, indicating she isn't performing at the level of the average or above-average students."

Abuela's face registered shock. "Excuse me, what do you mean?" she demanded. She refused to accept the results. As she sat there, visibly stunned, the Principal mentioned that my test scores indicated a learning disability. This did not sit well with Abuela. She argued that the exams were inaccurate and insisted on a change in my placement, which was not granted. If I wanted to start school, I had to accept the assigned classroom.

Determined to not see me in that tier, Abuela sought other options while I attended Wagner Junior High. Interestingly, she never acknowledged the learning disability; to her, it was simply incorrect, and that was that. She didn't inquire if I struggled with the exams or had difficulties with the material. Instead, she used her extensive network—gained from her community activism—to find an alternative.

She learned about a program at Cathedral High School, an all-girls school on 56th Street and 1st Avenue. The program paired students with mentors who would sponsor their tuition for four years. Spots were limited, but Abuela acted swiftly, securing me a place. I didn't know the details of her negotiations, but I was relieved to be leaving the third-tier classes behind. One thing about her, she had the faith of a mustard seed. When she was determined to get something done, she was going to do it. She was a teacher of many lessons in my life. She believed that things were going to happen and she would fight until it was true. So, she was determined to get me in a school that could help me and develop me.

This is how I met Maureen, a New York City stockbroker who, having never married or had children, chose to give back through this program. We formed a lifelong bond that continues to this day. As a freshman at Cathedral High, I was delighted to reconnect with old friends from Mary Help of Christians, making my experience as a Cathedralite invaluable. I remain friends with many of the girls from that school to this day.

Abuela was also obsessive about skincare. She instilled in me the importance of applying lotion daily, not just on my body but also my face. Her advice proved invaluable, as I now frequently receive compliments on my skin's softness and appearance.

Despite our differences, I loved her deeply.

As a teenager, I was eager to hang out with friends, but Abuela was old-school—she went to bed at 6 PM and rose at 5 AM. I had to be upstairs when the lights came on for sure. If you know, that means when the night lights came on in the neighborhood, I had to be upstairs...most days. However, that was never good enough for me. There were days that I just had to be outside all night. I got slick and figured out when she would go to sleep, I could just sneak out while she was sleeping. This became a regular habit for me, I was able to sneak out many nights and make it back in before she rises, until that one night she got up to go to the restroom and realized I was not in the bed. That morning, I stuck the key in the door as quietly as I could and opened the door. There she was, sitting right there on the couch. She let me have it, with all her tiny might self, she started whaling on me. I was so shocked but one thing I was not going to do was hit my Abuela back. I remember sneaking out while she slept, only to be caught one night. When I returned, she was waiting for me, and her tiny hands with red nails smacked my arm until I was bruised. Now, my daddy, him and I would go at it, because he instilled in me that idea that "don't let nobody ever touch you". ...but that definitely didn't apply for her. I knew if I did anything out of line, I was going to have hell to pay with my Aunts and my Dad. That was the last of my days sneaking out. One thing about my Abuela, she was going to tell everybody she knew about what you did. She announced my misbehavior to anyone who called the house that day, no matter the reason for their call. It was her way of handling things. When I say everybody, I mean everybody, the mailman, the janitor, the neighbor, the grocery store manager, etc. She was big on telling on you, but I guess that was her way of embarrassing you, so you never do anything again. ha! She had her ways. I still miss her, and her passing during my college years left a void. Processing that grief has been ongoing, especially as I've faced more losses in my life.

College was a time of joy and independence for me. By my senior year, my father had reentered my life, cleaned up his act, and was visiting me regularly. He even took me to his apartment in Yonkers on weekends. He had turned his life around and never went back. I was proud of him and the life he was able to create for himself after getting past addiction.

Reflections of Faith:

What would we do without our grandmothers and abuelitas? They are often the driving force in our lives, providing strength and courage to become the people they believe we can be. They are our biggest supporters and advocates. Abuela's faith in me led her to fight for a better position for me, despite others' opinions. She saw potential where others saw limitations. We may not always value their efforts in the moment, but looking back, I wish I had told her how much I loved and appreciated her. She taught me invaluable lessons about life, from paying bills to skincare, lessons that continue to benefit me.

We all have special people in our lives who have impacted us profoundly. Take the time to express your appreciation and love for them while they are still with us. Everyone has an expiration date, and we never know when it will be. Honoring those who care for us is a sign of good character.

Who's the person or persons in your life who fought for you?

The person whose input you value the most?

Have you shared with them what they mean to you?

Write their name here, and if they're gone, take a moment to note how special they were to you.

Mike Murdock famously said, "You will be remembered in life for two things: the problems you solve, or the problems you create." In life, if you can solve problems without causing havoc or chaos, you will be seen as valuable. You are worth more to others when you know you have value to offer.

How are you solving problems in your life?

Symone'

Abuelita & Grandpa

Alvin S. King

Carmen (Candy) Mercado

Sharen

Shareen and Romaine

Brothers

Shareen and Tio Dad and Titi Mom

Mom with her children

CHAPTER

EIGHT

Unbreakable City Girl

I was so excited to start college; it had been quite a journey to get there. The admissions tests were challenging for me, and I didn't score well on the SAT and other entrance exams required for my first-choice university. As a result, I had to attend a secondary school before gaining admission to a university. I was disappointed, especially since many of my friends had been accepted into schools I couldn't get into. I now understand that testing wasn't my strength, but at the time, it was hard not to feel discouraged. If I had known about my learning disability then, it might have eased my self-criticism.

Despite the setback, I made it into a university! The sheer joy of being on campus and living independently as a young adult was exhilarating. My campus was decent—nice enough to make me, a city girl, feel like I was living in luxury. I had my own room, which felt like having my own apartment. I enjoyed attending classes and studying with the friends I made on campus. The freedom to attend parties and events without needing parental permission was fantastic. Although I missed my high school friends, who were only 40 minutes away by Long Island Rail Road, I planned to transfer to their school after my first year.

I was close enough to visit their campus and the contrast between their school and mine was striking—lush grounds, spacious dorms, and an impressive campus left me awestruck.

The first semester was manageable academically. I was focused on achieving a GPA that would allow me to transfer to the school where my friends were. I made some friends, including a group of guys who were part of the Omega Psi Phi fraternity. Known for their camouflage and wild reactions to the song "Atomic Dog," they became a part of my college experience. I was also interested in joining Delta Sigma Theta Sorority, Inc., and I observed the fraternity's activities to learn more about the process.

One of my friends, Tavio, looked like a younger Erik Estrada. He was a mix of Italian and Black, and although many girls were interested in him, we had a genuine friendship. During his pledging process, I would sneak him food to help him through. Tavio would later play a crucial role in saving my life.

I also met Mike, a charismatic gym enthusiast who was well-respected on campus. He started walking with me between classes and helping with groceries. Our relationship quickly turned into dating, but I soon realized he was possessive. He wanted to know my whereabouts at all times, showed up unannounced, and introduced me to his family, which indicated his serious intentions. I didn't feel the same way, so I tried to end things, but our campus was small, and that wasn't easy.

When I finally told Mike that our relationship wasn't going to progress, he reacted poorly. He threatened me, but I didn't take his threats seriously. One day, after shopping, he insisted on helping me carry my groceries to my room. Despite my protests, he followed me and refused to leave. When I asked him to go, he grabbed my keys, opened my door, and came inside. We argued, and he became violent. He choked me while professing his love, and despite my attempts to defend myself, he overpowered me. I eventually managed to grab the phone and hit him, but it only fueled his rage. He knocked me out.

I'm not sure how long I was unconscious, but I heard the commotion and saw Mike fleeing through my window. My friend Tavio heard all the commotion because he lived underneath my room, he must have rushed upstairs and fought with Mike and scared him off. Tavio then carried me into an ambulance. I remember the EMTs trying to stabilize me, and when I woke up in the hospital, my father and uncle were there. My face was swollen, my eyes black and blue, and my lips were swollen, which was horrifying. I also discovered a chipped tooth that had scratched my throat.

After being discharged, my father and uncle attempted to find Mike, who was on the run. I stayed in the car, not wanting to be involved. Thankfully, they didn't locate him.

I spent the following weeks recovering at home and seeing an ear, nose, and throat doctor for my throat issue. The chipped tooth had caused irritation, which was a relief to discover. I initially thought I had a tooth stuck in my throat, but it was just scratched. Eventually, my father took me back to campus, and the incident expedited my transfer to the university where my friends were. Despite the traumatic experience, God made a way for me to leave earlier and end up where I truly wanted to be.

Stony Brook University was transformative for me. Located on Long Island, just before Montauk, it was near the Hamptons, though we rarely explored the area. My time at Stony Brook was marked by forming lasting friendships and joining Delta Sigma Theta Sorority, Inc. I pledged the Pi-Delta chapter, and these women have been my steadfast support for over 30 years.

At Stony Brook, I was involved in student government, security teams for events, and concert promotions. These roles gave me invaluable experience in entertainment and organization. I developed a close relationship with Dr. Fred Preston, the Vice President, who became a mentor and advisor. I worked in various campus roles, which provided financial support and prepared me for a professional career.

Dr. Preston invited me to be a founding member of a new master's program in Student Community Development, focusing on community diversity initiatives. Being part of this program was a significant achievement and contributed to my professional development.

My time at Stony Brook taught me a lot about myself, including leadership and the importance of having a supportive community. Joining Delta Sigma Theta was a pivotal moment. I had admired the sorority since high school through the Upward Bound program, where I was first introduced to these incredible women. and was eager to join. Though I initially thought it would be easy, the experience proved challenging, but I ultimately became a Delta.

Through all these experiences, I learned to be a leader, a sister, and a friend. Despite carrying past hurts and traumas, my faith and support system helped me persevere. Being part of the Gospel choir provided an outlet for worship and gratitude. Reflecting on my journey, I see God's grace in overcoming adversity and growing through challenges.

Reflection of Faith:

I've come to realize that I'm built differently. Surviving my early college years without being broken or defeated is a testament to God's grace. He provides healing and fills our hearts despite past hurts. The experience taught me to be cautious and discerning, recognizing red flags and building a supportive tribe around me.

Questions for Reflection:

What past hurts have you experienced that you believe God has healed you from?

In what areas of your life have you felt God's grace carrying you through?

Scripture:

1 Peter 5:7: "Cast all your cares upon God, for He cares for you."

Ephesians 6:18: "And pray in the Spirit on all occasions with all kinds of prayers and requests. With this in mind, be alert and always keep on praying for all the Lord's people."

CHAPTER

NINE

Your Life is a Highlight

While I was working at The Brook, I made several valuable contacts in the entertainment industry. One of the notable connections was with Andre' Brown, who managed the Uptown Comedy Club in Harlem and was also the creator of a television show that aired on Fox. He presented me with numerous opportunities to interact with comedians who would later become major stars. I remember him asking me to bring Tracy Morgan to our campus for a show, and true to his word, it was an incredible event. Andre' taught me a lot about running a club, working with comedians, and organizing shows.

Another unforgettable performance was by Leaders of the New School—Busta Rhymes, Charlie Brown, Milo, and Dinco D. They absolutely brought the house down. The night was like the ultimate house party you could imagine. We also had the Fugees—Lauryn Hill, Pras, and Wyclef—perform, which was another major highlight. These experiences helped me build a strong network in the entertainment and music business by the time I graduated.

One of my closest friends, who remains a friend to this day, is Lelee from the iconic R&B group Sisters With Voices (SWV). Although I don't recall exactly how we met, I remember that she said I reminded her of a friend named Natalie. When I learned who Natalie was, I felt honored, as she was a beautiful person and one of Lelee's best friends. Tragically, Natalie passed away shortly after we met, having been hit by a car while standing at a payphone. It seemed that God had brought us together during a time when Lelee was grieving the loss of a close friend. We bonded instantly and became inseparable.

At the time, SWV was signed to RCA Records, and I spent so much time with Lelee that people assumed I worked for the label. They would ask me to help organize events and handle various tasks at the office. Eventually, due to issues with their management, SWV signed with Flava Unit Entertainment, a management company owned by Shakim Compere and Queen Latifah. Flava Unit managed several hip-hop groups and artists, including Monica, Outkast, Faith Evans, Total, SWV, Groove Theory, Monifah, Gina Thompson, LL Cool J, Zhané, Donell Jones, and Naughty By Nature.

When SWV joined Flava Unit, they were affectionately referred to as "the girls." Lelee was seen as the wild card of the group—known for her candidness, love for fun, and unpredictable nature. We were like two peas in a pod, always out and about, enjoying our freedom. However, Lelee wasn't much of a morning person, which sometimes led to her being late for recordings or meetings. The management team struggled to keep track of her whereabouts, so they offered me a job to help manage her schedule. Since we were together all the time anyway and they knew I was reliable, it made sense for me to step into this role. That's how I began working for Flava Unit.

I remember Michael "Blue" Williams, who was one of their road managers at the time. He would travel with many of their artists and later went on to manage Hip-Hop legends like Outkast and Andre 3000. One day, he pulled me aside and asked, "Can I count on you to keep her on schedule?" I assured him I could, and that's how I officially became an employee of Flava Unit Management.

Our first tour together was the Keith Sweat tour, with Kut Klose and SWV as the female acts. It was a blast, and we spent most of that summer on the road with a fantastic group of dancers and crew. During that time, I met one of my closest friends, Merylin Mitchell, an all-star dancer who performed with legends like New Edition, Mary J. Blige, Bobby Brown, Whitney Houston, and Michael Jackson. Although she was on a different tour, we occasionally crossed paths.

Life was exhilarating; we were traveling and working, blessed with incredible opportunities. After the Keith Sweat tour, we joined the Magic Johnson tour, headlined by R. Kelly. Meeting Magic Johnson was a highlight—he was gracious and generous. Over the years, there were many memorable moments, like when SWV was asked to contribute to the "Men In Black" soundtrack with Will Smith. I remember Will Smith organizing a private movie theater night for his team to celebrate the film's premiere. Jada Pinkett, who was pregnant at the time, was there. Will Smith rented out the entire theater, with catered food and treats. It was a classy gesture, and I was impressed by his thoughtfulness.

One standout moment was attending the Grammys when the "Waiting To Exhale" album was nominated. Sitting behind Prince and his wife was surreal. He looked like a living doll and an angel combined. The album received 11 Grammy nominations and won Best R&B Song for Whitney

Houston's "Exhale (Shoop Shoop)." Watching Prince up close and observing his interactions with his wife, Mayte, was magical. I've rarely been star-struck, but Prince and Michael Jackson were exceptions—though Michael Jackson is a story for another time.

Working with Flava Unit and getting to know Queen Latifah on a personal level was life-changing. Most of us called her "La" for short, but I affectionately referred to her as "La-quita." At the time, she was gearing up for her major film, *Set It Off*, directed by F. Gary Gray. I remember the excitement of flying out to LA for the premiere. We stayed at her Toluca Lake home for the week of events. Although I mistakenly wore a cream-colored suit instead of black, La found it amusing, and we laughed it off.

On the night of the premiere, La and Shakim had everything planned out. Several low riders picked us up and took us to the famous Chinese Theatre. The red carpet was rolled out, and everyone was excited to see the film. We were all a bit nervous about La's character's fate in the movie, and when the dramatic moments came, we reacted passionately, even though we knew it was all fiction. It was a proud moment, seeing La as a real movie star.

The after-party was equally enjoyable. I remember La introducing me to an actress who played a prostitute in the movie. Instead of simply saying hello, I blurted out, "Oh, you were the hoe!" La burst out laughing, and I tried to clarify my comment, but it was clear what I meant. We had a great laugh, and La joked that she might not introduce me to anyone else again!

We had so many fun nights in Hollywood. We were a pretty wild crew, always ready to have a good time. I remember one night in particular; Da Brat threw a birthday party in Hollywood. It might have been the same week we were there, though I can't recall for sure. The party was announced on the radio, remember when they used to do that? That was always a sign that a party was going to be epic!

A bunch of us showed up at the party like a mob. Back then, you'd often find a camera crew capturing the night, much like Ralph McDaniels on 'Video Music Box'. The venue was packed with artists and celebrities. During the party, people were asked to say something special for Da Brat's birthday, sharing their love and best wishes. Da Brat was always cool and friendly, with a great demeanor.

When the mic came to Lelee, my girl from SWV, we all braced ourselves. Lee was known for her unpredictability and her straight-shooting style. She wished Da Brat a happy birthday and added some other comments. I won't share what she said, but let's just say my reaction was, "Oh-my-God, Lee! You can't say that!" If anyone finds those clips, burn them! A few of our friends were red-faced and in disbelief at what she had said on the mic. That's our Lelee, and we love her for it.

Reflection of Faith:
You never know what door is going to open for you, so be helpful and show yourself as an asset, not a liability. Keep learning and don't shy away from a job you feel unqualified for. No job is too small or too big. Remember, favor is not fair. As Mike Murdoch said, people will remember you for either the problems you caused or the problems you solved. The person who can solve problems is always the most valued and often the best compensated.

I know that God has always taken care of me, opening doors and providing opportunities that I often don't fully understand. I trust Him to guide and lead me, so I don't worry about anything. Here are a few scriptures to stand on when you're believing for God to open doors for you:

Philippians 4:6: "Don't be anxious about anything—make your requests known to God."

Proverbs 16:7: "When a man's ways please the Lord, he makes even his enemies to be at peace with him."

Luke 2:52: "Jesus grew in wisdom and stature, and in favor with God and man."

CHAPTER

TEN

A Place to Breathe

Working for Flava Unit was life-changing. When La was offered the opportunity to have her own talk show in NYC, she wanted to give us all a chance to work on it. None of us knew much about TV production, well, let me speak for myself, I certainly didn't. Nevertheless, we had to interview for the job. At the time, Cathy Chermol, a TV executive, was the Executive Producer of the show, and our interviews were with her.

I remember thinking that this was quite different from the music business, which we called "the industry." In music, we didn't really dress up; a lot of our business was conducted in streetwear. So, I figured I'd better get an outfit to look like a professional. I went to Banana Republic, thinking it had the most professional-looking outfits. I bought a gray sweater dress with a matching cardigan and paired it with knee-high gray boots from Nine West. At the time, I was also obsessed with Tiffany & Co., well, I actually still am. For the interview I treated myself to a signature bracelet with the aqua blue heart to complete my basic office-girl look.

Excited for my interview, I showed up and was thrilled to meet Cathy. To my surprise, we were wearing identical outfits! I couldn't believe it. We even had some matching Tiffany jewelry. It was a funny moment that made me realize I'd dressed like an older woman—an outfit I would never wear again. Despite the wardrobe mishap, Cathy loved my personality and offered me the job. Just like that, I was an Associate Producer. I was terrified; the responsibilities seemed immense, and I was unfamiliar with what lay ahead. But Cathy was confident in my abilities, and that confidence gave me a boost.

The job was one of the hardest I've ever had, and I've had my share of tough jobs. It was a fascinating time, filled with intense learning experiences. I worked with a remarkable woman named Evolyn Brooks, who would later become my lifetime friend, sister, and mentor. Together, we brainstormed show ideas, including one called "Ladies First," inspired by Queen Latifah's hit song. We invited trailblazing women like Theresa Weatherspoon, Vickie Johnson, Kim Hampton, and Laila Ali. These women would become my friends in the years that followed.

We also had an amazing talent show idea, inviting celebrity artists to judge raw talent. I'm convinced we came up with the concept for American Idol before it existed, but we missed the opportunity.

Our team was fantastic. We worked incredibly hard, putting in hours that would be unacceptable in today's work culture. During my year on the show, my dad was very ill, which affected me deeply. The job became increasingly tough as I tried to maintain excellence while dealing with my dad's declining health. I knew I couldn't continue like this for another year. I often worked until 4 a.m., sometimes overnight. I joined a gym next to our studio just to shower. Despite loving my colleagues, I knew I needed to address my father's health.

At the end of the season, Jim Paratore, President of Telepictures, would occasionally come to our offices to check on the show. He would pride himself with chatting up the staffers and getting to know you. He was a great man and well respected. He has since passed away, tragically he had a heart attack while riding a bike in Paris, France. He was only 58 years old at the time, but I can't even image how much stress it could be to be in charge of such a large production company. I was extremely stressed over and with the work load of the job.

One day, he came into my office and asked how I was doing. I told him I was struggling with my dad's illness. Jim, serious and compassionate, advised me to spend time with my family. He said, "You only have one family; maybe you should go spend some time with your dad." Exhausted from work, I wasn't sure what to do. I was so shocked that those words came out of his mouth. I eventually left the job that season, though I was on the brink of being fired. I went to see my dad, who had moved to Palm Bay, Florida to escape New York's weather and be closer to his sister, Denise. I'd visit her often, and flights from New York to Melbourne, Florida, were inexpensive on Spirit Airlines.

I spent that summer visiting my dad and brother, Ryan, and it was a relief. After returning to New York, I wasn't sure what to do next when my friend VJ called. Like I said, earlier, we had become great friends after meeting. She was playing for the New York Liberty at the time, but during the winter breaks she would regularly travel overseas to play during her breaks from the league. Her mom was at risk of losing her leg, and VJ was considering leaving the league for a bit to care for her. I offered to help her mom while VJ continued to play. I packed a bag and headed to Coushatta, Louisiana. I enjoyed the small-town lifestyle, and the sign reading "Home of Vickie Johnson" made me smile. At that time, the town had little in the way of commercial stores, and the excitement over a new Burger King being built there was palpable.

I fell in love with Susie Marie Johnson, VJ's mom, who was also known affectionately as "Rie". She was one of the sweetest, funniest, and kindest women I'd ever met. She loved casinos, which she referred to as "the boat." I quickly learned that "the boat" was a casino on an actual boat, and going there was a big deal for her. I enjoyed spending time with her and learning about her lifestyle.

During my stay, I had ample time to reflect and work out. I rode VJ's bike around town, often getting stares from all the locals trying to see who I was, because everyone knew everyone in town! I also often got lost but always finding my way back, because honestly the town was about a 10-block radius, if even that. VJ's grandmother, Madea, was a character, a no-nonsense woman with a gun in her purse, just like Tyler Perry's Madea. I ran errands for her and noticed her deep faith. She would have Benny Hinn or other televangelists on TV and send small donations for prayer cloths or healing. She would often ask me to mail out her request occasionally, I loved chatting with her. Her strong faith and love for God were evident and deeply impactful. Don't come into her yard without letting her know, if you were a man or an animal, you might catch a bad one.

While I was in Coushatta, everyone knew who I was and where I was staying. I used VJ's car to get around, though I only had a driving permit. I decided to take the driving test while I was there. I was studying so hard for the written and driving tests. I had to study for the written test and I had to take the driving test. I figured I would study for a week and then go take the test. However, I'm a terrible test taker, so I actually didn't feel confident in taking that test, until a whole month later. I was studying my butt off to memorize the information in the book. Rie was watching me study all the time and taking the practice test, which I couldn't seem to nail it. Finally, I got the courage to go take the written and driving test. I actually drove myself to the

DMV, how crazy was I. Anyway, I took the written test, and passed, I thought it was a miracle. It was time to take the driving test, and I was so nervous because I wanted to make sure that I didn't miss any street signs. When we pulled back to the DMV, the instructor said I passed. I was so happy. I took my picture and got my license, woohoo. Despite my anxiety about testing, I eventually passed the written test and the driving test, or so I thought. I later learned that VJ's mom had some influence in town and had ensured I received my license, regardless of the driving test outcome. It was a reminder of how valuable connections can be and how friends in high places can make a difference.

I was grateful for everything Rie did for me and for our time together. She helped me in ways she couldn't have known. We really had a chance to get to know one another, and she taught me a few things about cooking and decorating. She loved to decorate; she was the Queen of a tchotchke! I appreciated our time together, although she thought I was there for her, she really helped me more than I could ever articulate. I was filled with love and hope while I was there. Through that sacrifice, God gave me what I needed to prepare me for what was coming. I was filled with love and hope, and the experience prepared me for what was coming.

I stayed in Coushatta for several months to help Rie get adjusted to her new life in a wheelchair. The time was invaluable to me, I was able to spend a lot of time alone to process and think about what was happening in my own family. I was there without distractions, I didn't know anyone, I didn't have anywhere to run to be distracted. I had to be present where I was, because someone else was relying on me. There were many nights unbeknown to Rie that I spent crying myself to sleep. I was definitely in a broken place in my life, but I didn't have the capacity to recognize it at the time. So, it was an escape and a place where I was able to breathe and rest. I was so exhausted from working and so emotionally exhausted from knowing that my Dad was dying. I wasn't quite ready to deal with everything head on, but before I knew it, I was going to be forced to.

My time in Coushatta was a much-needed escape and a place to breathe and rest. It allowed me to process and reflect on my family situation without distractions.

Reflection of Faith:
God placed many people in my life to show me the love of a mother. Though I didn't have my own mother, I experienced a mother's love through my grandmother, aunts, mentors, and women assigned by God to nurture me. God cared for me deeply, providing these experiences to impact my life.

Two lessons emerged from this time:

When life feels upside down, sometimes you need to find a place to breathe, even if it's unfamiliar. Don't be afraid to step into the unknown; you may find something beneficial there. *Genesis 12:1-2*
"Now YAHWEH said to Abram, 'Leave it all behind—your native land, your people, your father's household, and go to the land that I will show you.'"

Being of service to others can open the door to your own healing. Putting yourself aside to help someone else can help you see past your own problems and invite God's intervention. The greatest gift we can give one another is the gift of service. *Mosiah 2:17*
"When ye are in the service of your fellow beings ye are only in the service of your God."

Look for opportunities to serve others without expecting anything in return. Write down ways you can be of service this week and ask God to show you how you can help someone. He will guide you.

1 John 5:14

"If we know that He hears us in whatever we ask, we know that we have the requests that we have asked, if it's in His will."

CHAPTER ELEVEN

The Big Regrets

I received a call while I was in Coushatta from my aunt, and I could immediately tell something was wrong. She was very upset, and when I asked what was happening, she said, "You need to get to Florida right away. Your dad isn't doing well." I wasn't ready to hear that, and my response wasn't great. Still, I made plans to head to Florida. I caught a flight from New Orleans, and when I arrived, I was terrified to go to the hospital. When I finally walked into his room, my dad was no longer speaking. I don't remember if his eyes were open, but he was completely dependent on the machines keeping him alive.

I was numb and in shock. I knew this moment was coming, but it felt like I was losing yet another lifeline to who I was. At that point, I had already lost my mother, my grandmother, my godfather Bernard, and my little sister Symone'. I can't fully describe what that felt like at the time; all I remember is feeling numb.

I haven't mentioned this before, but after my dad got clean, he married a childhood friend and had two beautiful children with his wife, Romaine, Symone' and Ryan. Tragically, Symone' contracted HIV during conception, and her short life was a constant battle. Her body couldn't keep up with the medications, and at just 9 years old, her fight ended. A few years before my dad's death, I lost her, my sweet little babysitter, my baby sister. Her death devastated me, and her battle was kept quiet within half of the family. During that time, people were terrified of HIV/AIDS, and no one really spoke about it. Losing Symone' was crushing, but I suppressed my grief for years, unable to fully process the loss. Her death was kept hidden, and our family's pain was overlooked in silence, a full-blown exercise in avoidance.

Symone' died at 9, and I was 9 when my mother passed. I often think about that coincidence. I don't know if there's a connection, but it lingers in my mind. Her death affected my dad deeply too. We never talked about it, but I think he felt guilt over her passing. She was conceived out of love, but my dad had contracted the virus after he got clean. Everything seemed to spiral downward from there.

Back in that hospital room, sitting by my dad's bedside, I watched him struggle to breathe. Each breath seemed so painful. As I held his hand, I reflected on all the things I wished I had said to him. I was overwhelmed with grief and regret. It felt like I was watching the scene from outside my own body, floating above the moment. All I could think about was how to apologize for all the times I gave him grief, for being disrespectful and angry for most of my life.

When my dad got clean, I wasn't a good daughter. I was resentful, angry at the years of addiction, abuse, and absence. I took it out on him by being disrespectful, running away from home, and thinking I could do whatever I wanted. In the hospital, I regretted it all. I felt terrible for the way I treated him.

I had some time alone in my dad's hospital room. It was then that I begged for his forgiveness. I squeezed his hand, cried on his chest, and poured out my apologies. He couldn't respond, but after I spoke, I felt a sense of peace. I continued to cry uncontrollably, laying my head on his chest, holding him for the last moments of his life. It did something to me, like a part of me died with him. Memories of all the good things about my dad rushed back. He was a great dad who loved me the best way he knew how. He never had the tools or capacity to deal with the demons he faced as a child, but I know now that he did the best he could with me.

One thing I knew for sure, he loved me. He never left me, never forgot me, and never stopped loving me, even when I probably deserved it.

Listening to his last breath was painful. Even though I had known for years that his death was coming, it felt unreal when it finally happened. I wasn't ready. I had avoided him and his condition for so long, and now there was nothing I could do. The pain numbed me, and I felt like an orphan, even though my aunts loved me. Losing both of my parents felt like a loss of the people who made me, gone forever.

We buried my dad quickly, within a week. I was at my aunt's house in Florida, but I didn't feel like talking to anyone. The days blurred together, and I just wanted everything to be over. At the funeral, I sat off to the side, away from everyone. I didn't want anyone hugging or touching me. I wanted to be left alone. I know people were worried, but I was cold and distant. I buried the pain of losing my father, just like I had buried so much before. I ran back to what I thought was "normal" life, but nothing about my life felt normal anymore.

Reflection of Faith

John 13:7: "Jesus replied, 'You don't understand now what I am doing, but someday you will.'"

I believe my dad could have lived longer if he had dealt with the internal conflicts he was carrying—feelings of hate, resentment, and regret. But he didn't have the tools. His unresolved trauma led to addiction and poor choices. One of the biggest lessons I learned from him is that not healing your life's traumas can ultimately destroy you.

Grief, I've learned, is the price we pay for love. It never goes away. Even now, as my eyes fill with tears thinking about Symone', I realize how much suffering I carried because I didn't process my grief. It wasn't until recently that I learned to release that pain—through tears, writing, working out, and moments of stillness. I had to understand how loss shaped me, how it affected my relationships, and how I kept seeking love and validation because I never let the pain leave me.

If you don't process your grief, it will stay with you as an open wound. It won't disappear, but you can learn to manage it in a way that doesn't cause harm in other areas of your life. Don't avoid your feelings like I did. It took me 40 years to begin to heal, and I missed out on so much love and joy along the way. But it's never too late to start.

Here are some ways to begin processing your grief: these were helpful tools that I found on a therapy page about grief.

Acknowledge your pain: Let yourself feel. Don't say you're fine when you're not. It's okay to admit, "I don't feel great," or "I'm having a hard time right now."

Accept grief: Maturity comes when you accept the reality of loss.

Seek support: Grief is hard. Don't go through it alone. Find someone you can talk to—a friend, a professional, or even a group of supportive people.

CHAPTER TWELVE

Working with Tyra

After my time at the Queen Latifah Show, I built some amazing connections and friendships. Telepicture executives appreciated my work, so I was fortunate to be on their list for upcoming projects. My mentor and friend, Evolyn Brooks was hired as a Supervising Producer for their next venture: The Tyra Banks Show. I was thrilled for her—what an incredible opportunity and talent to work with! She would be moving from New York to Los Angeles for the gig.

Tyra was at the peak of her career as a runway model and TV executive, with her show "America's Next Top Model" enjoying great success. The news that she was starting her own talk show in Los Angeles was exhilarating. When Evolyn called and asked if I would come out to join the team, I responded with an enthusiastic, "ABSOLUTELY!"

I flew out to meet the other executives in charge of the show. Despite my nerves—my TV career was largely due to my connection with Queen Latifah and I lacked formal experience in television—I aced the meeting and interview and was hired as an Associate Producer for The Tyra Banks Show. The show was filmed at the CBS Television studio lot, right next to the famous Grove in LA. The Price Is Right also taped there, so every day was a treat seeing people lined up in their quirky outfits, hoping to be picked to be on the show.

Working with Tyra was an intense and relentless experience. Our team worked tirelessly to get the show off the ground. Despite the challenge, it was an incredible learning opportunity. I was amazed to discover that so many of our crew members were from New York. This was where I truly grasped the enormity of the effort that goes into producing a television show. Sleep was a rare commodity, and we worked every weekend without pause. Yet, Tyra was always in the trenches with us, often coming into the office on her days off. She would often bring us food; her favorite was Barbeque.

Our creative meetings were a whirlwind of activity, and we had Tyra's creative retreats where we developed binders of ideas. It was hard work but also a lot of fun. The great thing about working with Tyra during this period was our access to her ANTM (America's Next Top Model) crew. We had the opportunity to be creative with her team, including well-known models like Eva Marcille, Tocarra Jones, and Bre Scullark. They were our go-to girls, and working with them was always a pleasure. There was a sense of familiarity and camaraderie that persisted whenever I crossed paths with them.

One quirky aspect of working with Tyra was her nickname in the office: "BBQ." It was an alias that stemmed from her love of barbecue. She would sometimes have barbecue delivered to the office for everyone to enjoy, a thoughtful gesture that was appreciated by all.

Many of the producers and crew from that show remain my friends to this day. The daytime television community is a tight-knit one, where everyone seems to know each other. During my time at The Tyra Banks Show, I kept my apartment in NYC and frequently flew back and forth on red-eye flights. I never fully moved to LA; it was as if my spirit knew I wasn't meant to stay.

I became good friends with my producer, Becky, who was from the Midwest—sweet and incredibly smart. We spent a lot of time together, both on and off work. One day, she mentioned she owned a house, which I found astonishing. I was intrigued and asked her many questions about it. Eventually, she offered to connect me with her broker, and I eagerly accepted, even though I didn't fully understand what a broker did at the time.

The broker educated me on the home-buying process, and soon, I found myself approved for a mortgage. The amount was astounding, and I was both excited and overwhelmed. I began exploring homes on Zillow and eventually fell in love with listings in Charlotte, NC. The houses were spacious compared to what I was used to in NYC. I decided to visit Charlotte to check out the properties in person.

Landing in Charlotte, I was immediately captivated by the green, lush areas. The first house I saw didn't appeal to me, but the second one did. It was in a new community with a backyard, a pool, tennis courts, and basketball courts. I was smitten. That night, I couldn't stop thinking about the house, so I pulled out my checkbook and asked my real estate agent how much I needed to write to secure it. The agent was perplexed by my offer, explaining that I needed to make an official offer and write a check for earnest money instead. Despite my inexperience, I managed to get the house, though I later realized I had paid too much due to my lack of negotiation skills.

Upon returning to Los Angeles, I was surprised to receive a call from Tyra's executive producers informing me that the show was moving to New York. While this was fantastic news, I was deeply invested in making my Charlotte plan work. I loved the city's warmth and community feel, which was a stark contrast to my upbringing in low-income neighborhoods.

Without a car, getting around Charlotte was a challenge. I relied on walking to a nearby supermarket for groceries, which felt normal to me as a New Yorker but quickly became impractical. I eventually bought a car, though I was swindled in the process—putting down $4,000 on a Jeep Cherokee. Who does that! I had no idea how to buy a car and thought I had done something with that purchase. Ha.

With no job and no connections in Charlotte, I was in a precarious situation. My cousin Natalie Simmons, who's a gospel singer and has had several successful songs on air, she connected me with Melanie Pratt, a friend in the local radio scene, who became my gateway to meeting people and landing freelance gigs. Despite my efforts, I had to take a job at Belk's department store to make ends meet.

Just as I was settling into Charlotte, I received a call from Terry Murphy, a well-known TV executive from HARPO. She offered me a chance to join a team in New York for a test show with Nate Berkus, Oprah Winfrey's interior designer. Excited by the opportunity, I met with Terry in New York and was thrilled to get the job. Although I wouldn't be part of the Chicago team, I devised a plan to make myself indispensable. I convinced Terry that my skills in connecting with people and gathering leads were crucial for the Chicago shows.

After weeks of hard work and strategizing, I was able to secure a spot in Chicago. HARPO took care of everything, including shipping my belongings and arranging transportation. This experience underscored the importance of betting on yourself and speaking up for your talents. As Isaiah 40:8 says, "A closed mouth doesn't get fed; a closed Bible can't feed your spirit." My faith and persistence paid off as I found myself working at HARPO studios on Nate Berkus's new show, walking through Oprah's halls and even spending per diem money at the gift shop. In the infamous Oprah style, you get a gift, you get a gift, and you get a gift, everyone back home was getting a gift from the Oprah gift shop.

And just like that, I found myself at HARPO Studios working on Nate Berkus's new show, walking through the Oprah offices and meeting Oprah's staff. The opportunity to roam those halls was monumental for me; I was beaming with pride just being in the building. I even managed to visit the gift shop, spending every last cent of my per diem on Oprah-themed memorabilia. True to Oprah's style, I felt like I had to share the love, so everyone back home was getting a gift from the Oprah gift shop.

Our test shows went well, and we were soon up and running for the new season of "The Nate Berkus Show." The show was a grind—days blurred together, and we often didn't know if we were coming or going once the show started. It combined lifestyle with home design makeovers, which made it demanding like any startup. Despite the challenges, I remember it being an especially tough show to piece together. The best part was the friendships we forged, bonding over hard work and late nights, and getting to know the genuinely sweet host, Nate Berkus. He was laid-back and down-to-earth; I recall a night we went to a diner and ordered onion rings with gravy—something I never expected him to enjoy, but we devoured them with gusto. Those were the good old days; I wouldn't be eating like that nowadays.

Nate Berkus underestimated the workload of a daytime talk show. I remember him sharing that Oprah had suggested he start with one show a week or a half-hour show, but he was determined to handle a full daily show.

It was a grueling effort, and Oprah, who had been doing it for years, knew the toll it took. By the end of the first season, we were exhausted, and I felt my time there was up. The executive changes were confusing, and I felt unappreciated. I decided it was time to move on, even though I wasn't sure what was next.

I took a bus uptown to my apartment, needing some time to think. I wasn't much of a train rider—cabs and buses were my usual modes of transport. While on the bus, my cell phone rang; it was Joyce Coleman-Sampson. "Hey, Shareen, whatcha doin'?" she asked. I told her I had just quit my job at Nate Berkus. She responded, "Oh, good, because I need you to work on a new show with me called 'Bill Cunningham'." I hadn't even been unemployed for 24 hours! When I say God has been good to me, I mean it—He has always guided me from one opportunity to the next. Joyce said I needed to meet Kim, the EP of the show, and that we'd hit it off. Sure enough, when I met Kim, it was a great fit. She offered me a title two levels above what I had at Nate Berkus, with a salary that was impressive. Back then, talk show salaries were substantial because the work was demanding. The industry has changed significantly since then, but our run was memorable.

At BCS, I worked as a Senior Producer on a show focused on family conflict and drama. We aimed to help families reconcile or resolve issues. Our show was different from "Jerry Springer" in that we sought real-life resolutions rather than entertainment. Occasionally, we faced intense situations, such as one time when an entire family nearly attacked me on stage. We had a segment where we invited feuding neighbors from Ohio who had passed down their animosity through generations. Convincing them to come to New York was a challenge, with many nights of negotiations. On the show day, I invited my husband to witness what I thought would be an explosive episode. He had never seen my work before and was in for a shock.

During the show, things escalated quickly. The tension among the guests grew, and during a commercial break, I tried to mediate, but two daughters surrounded me and started waving their hands in my face. My husband, unprepared for the scene, jumped on stage to help me. Security quickly intervened, not recognizing him, and one of my Executives yelled at him to return to the audience. My husband yelled back, and I feared I would be fired. Looking back, it's a laughable moment, but at the time, it was serious. Our Executive Producers were highly respected, and any defiance was risky. I was fortunate to escape with just a warning, and new rules were put in place—no family members allowed in the audience.

Despite the chaos, I enjoyed working with Bill Cunningham. He was a cheerful and funny older man, and our small team was tight-knit and supportive. The show ended in 2016, but the bonds we formed remain strong.

Reflecting on my career, I feel grateful for the chance to help people, even in a conflict-driven show. There were positive outcomes, too. For instance, my girl, Lelee, from R&B group SWV, shared a story about a family member who discovered he had been switched at birth. Our show helped him find closure and understand his true family dynamics. We always aimed to provide answers and avoid exploiting our guests.

We also had fun with entertaining segments, like a talent show. I had the idea to bring in celebrity judges, and though we didn't secure Adrienne Bailon, we did have Monifah, Lady Gaga's and Beyoncé's music director Joe "Flip" Wilson, and Chisette Michelle as judges. It turned out to be a fantastic show.

After a five-year run, we were disappointed when Bill decided to end his contract. However, within days, Jason Kutz from the Steve Harvey Show in Chicago reached out with a new opportunity. I was thrilled and quickly moved to Chicago to work on "The Steve Harvey Show." My coworkers were amazed at how swiftly I secured a new job, but I wasn't surprised. I've always felt that God has been with me, guiding and providing even when I don't deserve it. Faith has been a cornerstone of my journey.

Reflection of Faith

Throughout my career, I've always sought to help others, and I believe that God has rewarded that generosity. Think about times when God showed up in your life at just the right moment, changing your situation overnight. When you focus on Him, He makes time for you. Things aren't over until God says they are, and He will open the next door for you.

Scripture: Luke 6:38: "Give, and it will be given to you. A good measure, pressed down, shaken together, and running over, shall men give into your bosom."

Maya Angelou: "People will never forget how you make them feel."

CHAPTER

THIRTEEN

It's a Blizzard!
(In more ways than one)

I was so excited to go to Chicago that I didn't even care how cold it was. My family loved Steve Harvey and was part of the 4.1 million Americans who watch Family Feud every night, so they were beyond excited. However, the first day I landed in Chicago, a blizzard hit, talk about timing. After all the trash I had talked about it not being colder than New York, I was proven wrong. When I arrived at O'Hare Airport, the runway was frozen. No joke, we had to sit on the plane for over an hour as they tried to de-ice the runway and the gates. I had never seen so much snow in my life, and that's saying a lot coming from New York. Everything outside was snow white. At that moment, I knew it was in for an adventure and it was going to be a fun and exciting time.

I was thrilled to be working with such a talented team of producers, many of whom I knew from my days at Tyra Banks. Some were new, but they were all among the best in daytime television, and it was going to be a treat to work with them. The production company was very generous, putting me up in a hotel until I found a place to live. I stayed in downtown Chicago, right in the heart of all the shopping and restaurants. I loved it there. It was like being in Manhattan, only a hundred times cleaner. I can't stand walking the streets of New York because of all the black garbage bags left out, if you know, you know what I mean... one of the biggest reasons why I moved out of NYC in the first place, but I digress. Chicago, you never saw anything like that. The streets were immaculate. I'm obviously only speaking about the downtown area, Michigan Avenue, where I was surrounded by Michael Jordan's restaurant, The Burberry Store, Chanel, and Louis Vuitton. I loved the stores but always hated shopping—I'm more of a get-in-and-get-out type of shopper. Still, I liked the idea of being surrounded by luxury.

The staff was very proud and everyone seemed genuinely kind, caring about each other's work. They were close-knit, with many traditions and superstitions. In fact, the EP, Alex Duda, had this superstition that if someone didn't make a bundt cake every week, the show would be a failure. I can't remember quite how the story began for her, but every week, we would gather in the office to see how someone was surprised with the responsibility of making a bundt cake for the entire staff. People ran from this responsibility like the plague, it was pretty funny. Not only did you have to bake a cake, but you also had to come up with a creative way to surprise the next person with the task. Although it was fun, it felt like a chore that no one wanted on top of their exhausting workload. Staffers got very creative with their missions; you'd leave your office to do your show and come back to find your entire office decorated with a note saying you got "bundt." Ha!

During my first week, I was observing a lot of things and was pulled into a few meetings to see how things were done. I shadowed a few producers, and I remember Alex calling me into a briefing with Steve for the first time. He came with a few people from his team. Alex introduced me as a new producer. Typically, I was used to briefing my host with the content of my show, but that's not how things were done here. Every place is different, but I watched Alex as she ran down the entire script for Steve. He listened the entire time and had a few questions at the end. He was curious about the segment I was assigned and asked me a question, I think I was shocked that he actually looked at me. Alex jumped in and answered the question. I don't think I've ever been stunned to answer a host before. Steve had such a huge presence and looked you straight in the eye when he spoke to you. It was a bit intimidating.

Steve Harvey was a force, so witty. Our briefings were always interesting. Let me back up; in Chicago, we didn't really have private briefings with him. It wasn't until later, when he took his show to LA, that we spent a lot more individual time with him. However, in Chicago, the time we spent with him on the floor while taping was always hysterical and educational for us as producers. We got a better sense of him as a host and individual. He seemed to really enjoy helping people find love and their passion in life. I found that he was also a very sensitive man, tapped into his emotions. He cried a lot on the show, and the audience loved that he wasn't afraid to show his real emotions.

We had a lot of fun producing that show, coming up with so many creative themes and ideas. It was one of the most creative staffs I've ever worked with. There was Love Month, Jump Week, geared after Steve's best-selling book, 'Jump', and Crowd Sourcing, where we used friends and family members to help people struggling with love find it. Steve was known as the Chief Love Officer, and he took that responsibility seriously. We had a number of celebrities on the show to promote their upcoming projects and share about their recent ventures. We always loved having Steve's family on as guests, it was nice to see him with his family, and they were always willing to accommodate us. I remember working on our "baby shower hour," a show dedicated to his oldest daughter, Karli, having her first child. That was a great show, a lot of work, but a great show. We had an audience of pregnant women, and pretty much every gift we had on the show, we gave away to the audience members. I remember one of our PAs dressed as a stork, you know, like the birds that deliver babies. Ha! Every time he walked out on set, we rang some baby bells, and he would announce what gift everyone was getting. God bless him for participating in this show and going all out to make it great! We did some really fun and clever things on the show, there's a reason why it was an Emmy Award-winning show.

I had some great moments and memories of that show. I will never forget two big moments for sure. The first was when I was assigned someone who was an Oscar winner, featured in one of the biggest African American movies of all time. I was so excited to get the assignment. She was on the cover of Vogue Magazine and was coming on to promote her next project. The day of the show, I was super prepared. I felt like we did an excellent job on her research and had a great game idea to play with her and Steve. It was all genius in my opinion.

Well, the morning of the show, the actress showed up late. After arriving late, she requested another 20 minutes to get herself together. I obliged her request, grudgingly, because I knew that wouldn't go over well with my EP and host. Now, Steve wasn't the type of host who taped a show within an hour, we usually ran late on tape days because Mr. H, as we affectionately called him, loved to talk and take his time. He never rushed through a segment or a story. He always took his time coming to set, but when he came, we were ready to go. I prayed that this would be one of the days he would take his sweet time coming to set. Fingers crossed, I thought after telling the actress, "No problem."

During the time I was in her green room, I noticed her eyes were bloodshot red, as if she was recovering from a late night out and was trying to get over a hangover. One, I needed to make my EP aware, and two, I needed to try and stall to give her space. I went and told my supervisor and my EP; they were just as shocked as I was. When I went back to her room, I saw Mr. H in the hallway. I gave him a look like, "What are you doing out here?" He looked at me and could tell something was up. He went to the stage, and I rushed back to her room to go over the segment with her. I explained that we were out of time and had to get going, so I started briefing her for the segment. She immediately started saying, "I don't want to talk about that," or "Do we need to go over that?" Half of the items we wanted to discuss, she was not interested in. Yikes, I thought. What are we going to do? This is why it's always a good idea to overproduce a little because sometimes you never know when a celeb will kibosh your ideas.

Anyway, once I finished going through everything, she said she needed to change her clothes. I thought, "Oh my gosh, this day is never going to get started!" I ducked out of her room, and when I looked, Mr. H was leaving the set and walking back to his own suite! This was not good. He stared at me, shook his head, and I just nodded and said, "I'm sorry." I quickly explained to him that something was up with the actress and it was a bit out of my control.

She eventually got ready, and the show started. I was standing next to my EP while the segment was going, and all I could hear was her saying, "This is shit," "This is all shit." I just looked at her. She said, "I'm sorry, I know I'm being an asshole," and I just looked at her and agreed. The actress was a bit tight-lipped and didn't give up any interesting facts about her life or anything we had hoped for. We still had another segment to go! This was a two-segment feature, and I felt doomed. Thank God we had planned to play a game, at least that might be more fun. And thank God it was. We had this idea of them doing a face-off, each taking a turn sharing a personal story about themselves and having to guess if the story was true or a lie. They both told each other the most lavish and crazy stories we, or the audience, had ever heard. They both wanted to win the game and were so convincing in their delivery of the stories. The audience was dead silent, listening so intently. It was so good. Things turned around, and this was playing out excellently. Well, I can't share the stories they told because it would be so easy for you all to Google and find out who I'm talking about. LOL. Sometimes when you're producing, you win some and lose some. However, you have to take the good with the bad and just learn from it.

The next moment I will always remember was my very last show in Chicago. My guest was Patti LaBelle, who was coming on to sing a farewell song and perform for Steve and the audience. She was incredible to work with, right from the moment she arrived, she was very interested in knowing what we needed from her and what we would like her to do. The first order of business was a rehearsal. We went through the rehearsal, and everything was great, but Ms. LaBelle requested someone write the lyrics for her on cue cards because, baaaaby, she could not remember those words. We love us some Ms. Patti.

The day went off without a hitch. Everything was great. She spent a lot of the day just talking to me as we waited for things to get going. She was very generous with her time and wisdom, and I appreciated every moment of it. After her performance that day, she waited for me to grab her hand, and then we walked off the set together. She kind of rubbed my back, patted me, and said, "You guys have done such a great job here at the show. You should be proud of the work you've done. I'm so happy I could come and share this special time with you all and perform for Steve on the very last show."

I have to back up a little bit to talk about the months leading up to that last season. Things got tricky during the final year of Steve Harvey's show. There were rumors that our show was canceled and wouldn't be coming back for another season. There was also a huge viral story about Steve sending an email to the staff, asking us not to talk to him in the hallways, not to interrupt him, and to stop coming into his dressing room. Somehow, this email got out. Steve admitted to writing it but said it was meant for just one person, not the entire staff. However, it created a lot of dissension and confusion around the office. Staffers started chatting secretly with one another, having behind-closed-doors conversations about what was going to happen with the show. Ultimately, where there is confusion, there is chaos.

We discovered that Steve had made a deal to own the show and get the rights or that he wanted to own the rights to the show. I don't know all the details of what happened with the deal, but we knew that the Steve Harvey Show was ending for sure. What we all learned was that a new show called *Steve* was going to be happening in Los Angeles, and Steve would be in charge of his own show, which was something he wanted. So, all the producers started talking secretly again because everyone wanted to know if we would be invited to go to Los Angeles to be part of this new show. No one really knew who was going to be in charge or what was going to happen. We didn't know if our EP was going to be the EP of that show or if there would be a new EP. Everything was really hush-hush.

One day, I was on set working, producing my show, and Steve handed me a note on a blue card. The note said, "Would you like to go to Los Angeles? Yes or No." I almost started laughing immediately. It felt like I was in seventh grade again, and a boy was asking me out to see if I liked him or not. I started to answer him right away, and then he pointed to his mic on his chest, reminding me that everyone was listening—because, obviously, when you have a mic on, the entire control room can hear everything you're saying. He quickly told me to put the note away, and we'd talk later. I remember the stage manager, my friend Terrell, looking at me, and we just exchanged shocked looks. I couldn't fold up that blue card fast enough and tuck it inside my binder to get through the rest of the show. I was afraid of my EP seeing the blue card, afraid of other staffers seeing it, I just didn't know how to take that moment. So, I tucked it away in my binder and finished producing the rest of my show.

Later that evening, when I got home, I had the courage to take out the blue card again and look at it to make sure it said what I thought it said. Sure enough, it was an invitation for me to come to Los Angeles to work on his brand-new show in sunny California. A week went by, and I didn't mention the blue card to anyone. I ran into Steve in the hallway as he was coming to set, and he said to me, "Okay, don't wait too long, let me know what you want to do." I looked at him and thought, "Oh my gosh, I actually have to give this man an answer." I didn't want to get caught talking to him again because you never know when his mic is hot or not, so I decided to write my answer back to him on a piece of paper. I got a blue card, wrote my response, folded it up, and got it back to him. That's how I told him I would be happy to join him in Los Angeles.

The next time I saw him in the hallway, he said to me, "Please don't talk to anyone about the show in Los Angeles because not everyone is getting an invitation. If someone asks you about it, please don't speak about it." I said I understood and would keep it confidential. Meanwhile, we still had a whole season of shows to tape. As the season went on, a number of producers were asking each other, "Hey, have you heard anything about going to Los Angeles?" And every time someone asked, the answer was always, "No, I haven't heard a thing." This made me think, "Wow, everyone is doing such a good job of keeping this secret because clearly other producers have been asked to join him in Los Angeles and are doing such a good job of not revealing that they've been invited." This went on for the entire rest of the season, and no one ever said a word if they were going to Los Angeles or not. Once the season ended, it became clear who was invited and who wasn't, but we'll get to that later.

I loved Chicago. I loved being by Lake Michigan, especially the bike trails. Riding bikes along the lakeside became one of my favorite things to do. The lake looked like an ocean, it's so large. The cold in Chicago was indescribable. I don't even know what to say about it; it's more than just cold! That's frozen wind hitting your face with a wind chill factor that's brutal. I spent a lot of time walking through Millennium Park, in the spring and summer, that is. They had the most beautiful landscapes and flowers. In fact, there was a garden area right in the middle of the park, it was amazing. I discovered how much I loved plants and flowers in a garden setting. I'm not a big "buy a bouquet of flowers" kind of girl, but I do love to plant a bush or flowers in the ground. The parks were filled with sculptures, and there were always a number of free events offered. Between the music and food, you could catch a festival almost every week during the summer.

I especially loved all the varieties of restaurants in the area. There was no shortage of good eats. We were right off Michigan Avenue and Wacker. I'll never forget when I discovered Do-Rite Donuts, the first place where I ever saw fried chicken sandwiches made with two glazed donuts. I had never seen anything like that. It was delicious, but I only ate it that one time because it just felt wrong. However, their donuts were to die for, they were so good. They had so many different combinations. There were also a number of Michelin-star restaurants, and we tried them all. One thing I can say about Chicago folks: they know how to eat, and they love to drink.

In addition to discovering a lot of culture in Chicago, I also discovered Bill Winston Ministries. I loved attending that church; Bill Winston was so knowledgeable about the Word of God and understood so much of the Bible that I couldn't get enough of going to church to worship with other Christians and receive a word from God. His ministry focused on walking in faith, building your faith, and living a prosperous life. During my time there, I really learned how to see myself the way God sees me, with high regard, and how to hold on to the promises of God.

While attending his church, I truly learned the power of sowing a seed—not just a monetary seed, but also a seed of time, kindness, or speaking a word into someone who may need it. The principle of sowing and reaping became deeply ingrained in my life. I gained a new perspective on what a seed is, and during those years, I planted many seeds in the lives of others. As my time at that ministry came to an end, I felt that my season there was complete. I had learned all that I could, and it was time to move on.

With the Steve Harvey Show in Chicago canceled, it was time to go on hiatus—a time we all looked forward to. It's like being a school teacher: you work all season long, get the holidays off, and then, when summertime comes, it's time to play. Now, I had to plan my move to Los Angeles.

On the first day at the new show in Los Angeles, we had a meeting on the rooftop of Stage One, where we taped *Steve* at the Universal Lot in Universal City, California. I was expecting to see many of my former colleagues when I showed up. However, to my surprise, I didn't see any of them. I only saw one person I knew from Chicago, and I was shocked. I couldn't believe it. Steve always rolled with the same crew of people—he liked the familiarity and trust of his crew. So, I knew I'd see Terrell and Tanya, but I was surprised to see Jennifer, who I knew lived in Chicago and had her family there.

However, I was happy to see all of them; they were the only familiar faces, and I was glad to have them there.

This crew mostly handled walking the guests to and from the stage, managing the mics for our guests and Steve, and handling all the logistics involving the host. They were like a tight-knit family, and when one worked, the others worked too. I loved that about them. However, I was utterly shocked to be the only producer invited to join Steve in his new venture on his new talk show. I couldn't believe it. I couldn't wait for the day to end so I could call my family and tell them that no one else was there—it was just me. I tell you, when God's favor is on you, there is nothing or no one who can stop what He has for you.

That first season of *Steve* in Los Angeles was quite fun and interesting. Steve wanted to create a late-night show vibe for daytime, and he was so excited to get a desk like the late-night champions—David Letterman, Jimmy Kimmel, etc. However, his desk was huge and just stood out on our set like a sore thumb. People took jabs at that desk left and right because it was so big, but Steve didn't care; he was happy to have his own desk and feel large and in charge. There's nothing Steve Harvey does that is small—everything he does is big. So, having an oversized desk wasn't a stretch. It wasn't until Ellen started making jokes about how large his desk was that I think it started to get to him a little, and eventually, he decided to change the set, and we got rid of the desk.

We had some really great times on that show. It only lasted for two seasons, but we did our best to make it what Steve wanted it to be. During the last season, we discovered that Kelly Clarkson would be getting her own show and would fill in the spot where the *Steve Harvey Show* was. We also found out that their test shows were being taped on our same set. That was a big "ouch" moment.

Reflection of Faith:

When I tell you that God has equity with me, I mean it! He has come through for me time and time again. He has never let me down and has been a proven force in my life. He has given me things I never asked for or didn't even know I wanted. What I know is that you should never worry about anything in your life if you believe that God is for you.

The biggest thing I learned working with Steve is that sometimes in your life, you have to jump! Steve was a great example of faith; he understood what it means to take a leap of faith on yourself, regardless of the outcome. Steve pushed everyone to jump, he even wrote a book about it. You have to have enough faith in yourself and your dreams to move when God says move. The thing about God is that He gives us the desires of our hearts, so if you have a dream or a vision about something, God most likely put that in your heart.

What I know is that God doesn't bless us just for ourselves. The blessings He gives us are honestly to help and give to others. Everything I have is because of God, and I'm not ashamed to tell people that.

Psalm 145:19

He fulfills the desire of those who fear Him; He also hears their cry and saves them.
19 He grants the desires of those who fear Him; He hears their cries for help and rescues them.

Philippians 4:6-13 (NLT)

6 Don't worry about anything; instead, pray about everything. Tell God what you need, and thank Him for all He has done.

7 Then you will experience God's peace, which exceeds anything we can understand. His peace will guard your hearts and minds as you live in Christ Jesus.

8 And now, dear brothers and sisters, one final thing. Fix your thoughts on what is true, and honorable, and right, and pure, and lovely, and admirable. Think about things that are excellent and worthy of praise.

9 Keep putting into practice all you learned and received from me—everything you heard from me and saw me doing. Then the God of peace will be with you.

CHAPTER
FOURTEEN

From Candy's Girl to the King's Daughter

You have to show up for yourself. You have to pray for yourself. There is power in prayer and it can and it will change your life. Be present in your own life, don't let your mind take you out of the will for God. What I've learned is that the biggest fight of your life starts with the battle in your mind. An idol mind is the devil's workshop, Proverbs 16: 27-29. It's the truth. Prayer can be your saving grace that helps you make better decisions in your life, have better discernment, and keep aligned with what the purpose of your life is.

When you try to get ahead of God you take yourself out of alignment with his will for your life. Be patient and wait on the Lord, and everything does work out for the way it's supposed to. …just hold on to that. I haven't always been a great example of that myself. I have repeatedly thought that I was being purposeful by going after life and making things happen on my own without consulting God, because I thought I knew best. I discovered so many of my decisions have I did without praying and asking God for his guidance in advance. I went to college without praying and that didn't turn out well in the beginning. I landed in some relationships that weren't meant for me, again, I also didn't consult with God. A lot of times he will allow us to have what we asked for, but it's not what he wants for us.

However, because I had a foundation of God in my life, I was always able to talk to God and to still ask for his goodness and mercy to help me. I know that God has been with me all the days of my life, regardless of the good or bad days that I've had. I never let go of him and he never let go of me. Psalm 23:6 says, "Surely goodness and mercy will follow me all the days of my life. "That's one word that I know that I've stood out the majority of my life. You've got to find your own Word to stand on.

Every day you have to make a choice in your life, you are either going to feed your fears, or you decide you are going to feed your dreams. I spent many days wasting time feeding my fears, so I'm here to tell you that you can combat those fears by listening and reading the promises of God. You also can't out run or escape your traumas of the past; they will always catch up to you. You can try to ignore them if you want, but they will sneak up on you and confront you at the most unexpected time of your life.

God uses your past to get you to your future, so don't be embarrassed or ashamed of what you've gone through. I have no regrets about anything in my life because it all brought me to where I am in my life now. God has used all the trauma and lost I've had in my life to shape my character.

Maya Angelou said "when you know better, you do better". As I've grown and have made some of the same mistakes over and over again, I tried to learn what the lesson was. Not play a victim or try to understand why something happened to me, but instead understand what was the lesson. Live and grow. Be kind to yourself. Gain knowledge, wisdom, and understanding and your life will begin to have different meaning to you. I have learned that

I've had to unlearn the bad habits and relearn how I want to be. However, everything pain that I have endured, every hurt that I have suffered was in preparation for me to become the woman I am today. The running theme in every circumstance in my life is that God used every pain to bring me back to Him. If I never learned to look to God from such a young age, I really don't believe I would have been able to make it in my life. I have always understood that God's mercy and grace has saved me to my own demise. I paid a price to be who I am and where I am, but because I stayed stuck on the idea that all things are working for my good. I could never give up on myself or what I know that God has promised for me as a believer.

Proverbs 3: 5: Trust in the Lord with all thine heart, and lean not unto thine own understanding.

Keep your faith strong! Build it up every day. Read, listen, declare the Word of God and don't ever stop. You can be smart and that is great, but when you have the wisdom of God you move differently, you do things differently because you have a discernment attached to your smarts.

Don't ever give up on learning, you are never too old to start over or to begin living the life you want for yourself.

Psalm 92:12-15

The righteous shall flourish like the palm tree. He shall grow like a cedar in Lebanon.

Those that are planted in the house of the Lord Shall flourish in the courts of our God.

14 They shall STILL bring forth fruit in OLD AGE. They shall be FAT and flourishing.

A great quote I came across while studying was by a man named Alvin Toffler. I found it interesting that he was a New Yorker, he was a businessman known for his understanding around the digital revolution. I was attracted to what he had to say because of his name alone, Alvin. That's my Daddy's name. Alvin Toffler said

"The illiterate of the 21st century will not be those who cannot read and write, but those who cannot learn, unlearn, and relearn." Alvin Toffler.

Keep learning. Keep loving. Keep going. You got this! You are worthy!

About Author

Shareen King is a multi-talented powerhouse in the media arena, whose diverse skill set has propelled her to the forefront of the industry. As the President and CEO of The King's Daughter Media, Inc., she seamlessly blends creativity, leadership, and innovation to achieve unparalleled success.

With a portfolio boasting multiple Emmy Award nominations, Shareen's talents extend far beyond traditional boundaries. Her ability to not only produce compelling television content but also spot and nurture emerging talent sets her apart in a competitive field.

Shareen has worked with such talent as Queen Latifah, Tyra Banks, Nate Berkus, and Steve Harvey, Shareen's versatility shines through in every project she undertakes. Whether she's crafting captivating stories or orchestrating seamless productions, her multi-faceted approach ensures that her work resonates with audiences on a profound level.

Currently serving as Senior Producer for esteemed programs like Access Hollywood and Access Daily, Shareen continues to showcase her remarkable talents, proving time and again that true mastery knows no bounds. In a world where specialization often reigns supreme, Shareen King stands as a shining example of what it means to excel across multiple disciplines, inspiring others to embrace their own unique talents and pursue their passions with unwavering determination.

www.ingramcontent.com/pod-product-compliance
Lightning Source LLC
Chambersburg PA
CBHW032055150426
43194CB00006B/533